Economic Reform and a Liberal Culture

And Other Essays on Social and Cultural Issues

Tom Rubens

SOCIETAS
essays in political
& cultural criticism

imprint-academic.com

Copyright © Author, 2010

The moral rights of the author have been asserted.
No part of this publication may be reproduced in any form
without permission, except for the quotation of brief passages
in criticism and discussion.

Published in the UK by Societas
Imprint Academic, PO Box 200, Exeter EX5 5YX, UK

Published in the USA by Societas
Imprint Academic, Philosophy Documentation Center
PO Box 7147, Charlottesville, VA 22906-7147, USA

ISBN 9781845401870

A CIP catalogue record for this book is available from the
British Library and US Library of Congress

Contents

Prefatory Note	1
One	
Economic Reform and a Liberal Culture	2
The Protest Perspective and Meritocracy	6
The Relevance of Spengler Today	11
The 'Princess Casamassima' Problem	16
Multi-Culturalism in English Society	20
Political Revolutions in Complex Cultures	29
Two	
Determinism and Prescription	36
Compatibilist Freedom and Global Causation	39
Some Further Arguments for Determinism	43
What is Ethical Rationality?	49
Schopenhauer on the Basis of Morality	65
Bertrand Russell and James Thomson	78
Russell and Santayana	82
Santayana and Hardy	85
Santayana and Schopenhauer	88

Mill and Nietzsche	94
A Necessary Hardness	99
Secularism As Against Religion	102
Various	107
Comte's Continuing Relevance	112
Max Weber	120

Three

The Poetry of Matthew Arnold	127
The Challenge of Major Literature	136
Modern Literature: Some Challenges	141
Index of Names	148

Prefatory Note

The following group of essays is divided into three main sections. The first section deals with social, economic and cultural issues; the second with topics which are essentially philosophical; and the third with themes which are chiefly literary. Throughout, the viewpoint expressed is that of secular humanism.

Also, in the essays generally, I use mentalistic terminology to convey a number of points about attitudes and ways of thinking. However, I use such terminology only from linguistic convenience and as a *facon de parler*. My position on the mind-body problem is actually physicalistic, but, for the reason just given, I do not deploy a physicalistic vocabulary.

T.R., January 2009

Economic Reform and a Liberal Culture

Since the word 'reform' implies improvement, economic reform can be defined in broad democratic terms as changes to the economic system which benefit the majority of the population rather than a minority: which, at the very least, secure for everyone an income adequate to meet basic nutritional and health needs, and, beyond that, raise the general standard of living and ensure a more equal distribution of wealth. As part of such changes, there is reduction or complete termination of the self-interested exercise of economic power by certain individuals or groups over other individuals or groups. Economic reform is, then, essentially a process which increases material wellbeing and decreases dominative pressures of an economic kind. It aims at enlarging the dignity and integrity of every individual. (In this, it is intimately linked to political reform; the closeness of the economic and the political is fundamental and constant.)

Physical wellbeing and freedom from economic domination are such vital objectives that some people might think that they were the only really important ones. But of course they are not. Christ's dictum, "Man shall not live by bread alone" is only one of the most famous of the many statements about the importance to human beings of meeting needs additional to economic ones. That importance is, incidentally, in no way diminished by Brecht's averral, to the effect "Grub before ethics." Ethics remains pivotal even if in second place in the statement; also, one is tempted to ask how, in the first place, "grub" is to be produced and distributed without some pre-existing ethical system or at least social agreement.

The needs additional to economic ones are clearly intellectual, emotional, cultural, social. Many of these are linked to economic wellbeing, but are, emphatically, not the same as it. Very often, such wellbeing is the necessary condition for their satisfaction; and even though this is not always the case, most people would agree that extra-economic kinds of satisfaction and fulfilment are less likely to be achieved when the economic situation is precarious. So, some degree of material security is usually a definite advantage for development in other areas of living.

Its role as an advantage needs to be emphasized because there are unfortunately cases where the advantage is not taken: where the achieving of material security and prosperity leads to little more than that. Hedonism, complacency, self-indulgence and even chronic boredom are sometimes the chief fruits of that attainment. Hence, while economic betterment makes cultural development more likely, it by no means makes it certain. Economic advance may well be accompanied by psychic stagnation, including a merely consumerist mentality. These considerations remind us of Nietzsche's concept of the 'Ultimate Man', the uncreative conformist and complacent hedonist, and typical product of a society whose goals are primarily or exclusively economic. It is not going too far to say that psychic stagnation can be, in its way, almost as inimical to cultural vitality as can political oppression.

Of all forms that cultural fecundity can take, the richest—I would argue—is a liberal culture. In such a culture, differences of outlook, viewpoint and kinds of achievement are not only tolerated but positively welcomed. Diversity and variety are not only accepted but also preferred, encouraged, protected. They are seen as indispensable ingredients without which society would lack savour and spectrum.

Also, from the specifically intellectual standpoint, the wider the range of expressed views of which the individual can avail himself, the greater the possibility of his constructing a viable position of his own on the issue in question. Such availability is crucial in science and philosophy: a point nowhere better stated than by Mill in the mid nineteenth century. Freedom to pick and choose; to accept or reject, either partly or totally; to look for compatibilities, however slender, between positions which at first seem to be irreconcilable; to critique arguments and to examine carefully what is offered as evidence; to remain in doubt, where necessary: this liberty is vital to the inquiring mind seeking independence from dogma, prejudice, unquestioned assumptions and all forms of authoritarianism.

It is accurate to say that a liberal culture has obtained in certain areas of Western society for the last 150 years or so: approximately since the time when the unprecedented advance of science became the distinctive feature of Western culture. This is not of course to say that a liberal culture consists only or mainly of science, but it is to say that the entrenchment of science reinforces and extends the spirit of free enquiry and open-mindedness which is characteristic of a liberal culture.

At the same time, the phrase 'certain areas of Western society' must be emphasized. It is undeniable that enormous numbers of people in the West, as indeed world-wide, have in the past been barred from the chance of extensively participating in that culture. This has been due to social and economic deprivation. Limited access to formal education, long working hours, low pay and constant economic pressure have in effect locked out millions from the opportunity for in-depth engagement with ideas, intellectual and artistic movements, scientific advances, and the general life of the mind.

It is true that this situation, certainly in Britain, has been changing, especially over the last forty to fifty years. But it has not done so at a uniform rate,[1] and not to the extent that further economic reform is not needed, both for its own sake and for the cultural advantages it brings.

There is no reason why efforts at economic reform should not go hand in hand with those to preserve, enhance and amplify a liberal culture. What should be aimed at is a combination of general economic wellbeing and maximal latitude intellectually and culturally. It perhaps goes without saying that a liberal culture is not in any sense a 'class' culture; by its very nature, it transcends class outlooks. Hence, those seeking economic reform on the basis of a specific 'class' position are not committed to a liberal culture. Their perspective is exclusionary, unaware of the possibilities a liberal culture possesses. This inadequacy is chiefly due to failing to see people *fully as individuals* — that is, to give close consideration to the quality of their individual minds and sensibilities. Such omission[2] is clearly a hazard entailed by an over-collectivist outlook of any kind.

Given these observations, the project for economic reform should endeavour to liberate people as individuals. Though these people have in large numbers been socially and economically deprived, they are not for this reason to be rigidly defined in class terms; since

---

[1] See, for example, current (2008) figures which show that social and economic mobility in Britain is now at its lowest for 40 years.
[2] Also, this omission accounts for a large amount of the inverted snobbery which is sometimes found among those with a rigidly 'working class' viewpoint. Such rigidity debars most of what is, in fact, the West's great cultural heritage, in literature and the other arts, and in philosophy. Generally on the problems surrounding 'class' concepts and outlooks, more will be said in the next two essays.

it is only as individuals that they can reap the manifold and complex cultural benefits of economic emancipation. Also, it is only as individuals that they can form meaningful estimates of their own performances, as contributors to or commentators on, that complex and indeed challenging culture to which they have gained access.

The word 'challenging' is used advisedly. The massive intellectual demands of a liberal and completely open culture are implied in Popper's telling phrase, "the strain of civilization," and in Malraux's concept of "the imaginary museum" of accumulated knowledge and achievement whose vastness must be encompassed, as a matter of intellectual obligation, by the modern mind.

It should be added that the complexity of a liberal culture, even in the context where capitalism is the dominant economic system, is of such magnitude that extreme care is required in relating it to economics. That care is not shown by those who characterise the whole culture as one whose ruling ideas are those of the economically dominant capitalist elite. By contrast, if it is argued, more modestly, that hegemonic capitalism is *only part* of the liberal culture (and such an argument can viably be made, given the history of the origins of capitalism in the West), then it obviously can be said that this part is driven by ideas which are economically dominant. But, if so, it will have to be added that this part is by far the intellectually simplest component of the culture. At the same time, there is a completely alternative argument which can be made: that hegemonic capitalism is actually *not part* of the liberal culture at all, but only co-exists with it. The general implication of all these points is that the culture would lose little or nothing in intellectual complexity even if the economic system ceased to be capitalistic.

The Protest Perspective and Meritocracy

Even if the social groups which are now economically dominant in Western society—those representing the interests of big business and big finance—were to have their industrial, commercial and financial power removed, major problems would still remain. Firstly, there would be the continuing possibility of new groups emerging, with the aim of becoming dominant.[1] Secondly, regarding the people without this aim—who are, in fact, the vast majority—there would be a different kind of problem: the persistence of mass-averageness (intellectual, cultural, moral) and an accompanying mass-conformism.

The latter problem, like that of economically dominant groups, has always existed. Its perennial nature can be see from the following references to major writers and thinkers across the last four centuries: In the seventeenth century, Shakespeare, in a mildly disparaging manner, depicted the attitude of "the indifferent children of the earth ... Happy in that we are not over-happy".[a] In the nineteenth century, Schopenhauer described the majority as 'Fabrikwaaren der Natur' (Nature's manufactured articles). Also in this century, Mill wrote:

> The general average of mankind are not only moderate in intellect but also moderate in inclinations: they have no tastes or wishes strong enough to incline them to anything unusual, and they consequently do not understand those who have ...[b]

In the twentieth century, Santayana echoed Schopenhauer's view,[c] while Eliot spoke of the morally middling character of most people.[d] More writers could be referred to, but this selection is substantially representative.

It is a delusion to think, as many on the political Left do, that whoever is not a member of the economically dominant group is, actually or potentially, someone with a significant contribution to make in the intellectual, cultural and moral spheres. Some on the Left even speak as if it follows with logical necessity that being a member of

---

[1] See in particular the writings of Pareto and Popper on this problem.

the non-dominant group must mean possessing the capacity for such contribution.[2]

To argue that the non-dominant majority lacks significant capacities *qua* majority is *not*, of course, to argue the converse: that the dominant minority do possess them, *qua* minority. This is because the qualities in question are rare among human beings in general, whatever their social and economic status. It is, then, not a matter of identifying such attributes with social groups or large collectives of any kind. Even if one were to agree with the extreme Left-wing view that these qualities are totally absent from the dominant minority (in accordance with the argument that their absence is the very reason for the dominance of that minority in the first place), then one would still be forced to acknowledge that their presence in the majority is sparse, to be found only among a few exceptional individuals. Hence, one must speak of a minority of individuals who cannot be defined in sociological group terms: a minority scattered across the human species, consisting of people who think more extensively, respond more widely and deeply, and originate more things, than the majority do.

To insist on this point is not, as some on the Left might retort, to endorse, implicitly or explicitly, the existing socio-economic *status quo*. To aver the rarity of momentous capacity is simply to assert that it will remain rare *whatever* the socio-economic system. This assertion is perfectly compatible with an argument for completely changing the current system if the latter chiefly serves the economic interests of elites: changing it, then, to one without the economic hegemony of elites. The argument is grounded in the view that control of this kind leads to, among its many damaging consequences, an undermining of the intellectual, moral and cultural spheres, especially with regard to freedom of expression and publication. However, accompanying the argument will be, again, emphasis on the exceptional nature of major ability, at all social levels.

To this line of reasoning there are two obvious logical extensions. One is that, in a system not controlled by self-interested groups, those who are prominent politically and socially will either possess outstanding capacity themselves, or will place a high value on those who do possess it. The second is commitment to establishing true equality of opportunity: chiefly educational and cultural, but also economic in so far as this equality does not allow the emergence of

---

[2] To what extent this way of thinking derives from mid-nineteenth century Marxism is a question worth considering.

economically hegemonic groups. Overall equality of life-chances will of course maximise the development of all existing human potential, but especially that of exceptional capacity, with all the rich variety this engenders.

Inequality of opportunity is one of the most glaring forms of social injustice, and all intelligent protest against the latter has foregrounded the issue of this inequality. It is in fact only equalled in importance by the issue of inequality in civil, legal and human rights: ones with which it is closely inter-twined.

Once equality of opportunity has been established, it is, clearly, to be distinguished from equality of outcome. Protest and rebellion are fully justified when they seek the former, but not when they seek the latter. To try to impose uniformity of performance—or, at any rate, to draw a line above which performance is not to rise—is unjust and illiberal in the extreme.

Hence all efforts at social reform and, where necessary, revolution, should be founded on an open-ended perspective and a commitment to an open society. That this has unfortunately not been the case with many of the social upheavals and revolutions throughout history, is a fact to be continually borne in mind. In so many cases, especially in the twentieth century, rebellions against a closed system have led to new kinds of social closure and authoritarianism—sometimes ones even harsher than those they replaced. The danger of such an outcome is on-going, attaching even to the most well-intentioned radicalism when the latter's social perspective is under-informed. An open society means a richly textured social and cultural fabric, an intricate and manifold cultural heritage, plus a full awareness of these facts and an actual welcoming of them.

Such complexity is intimately connected with exceptional ability. Without recognition of the latter, there is a simple, level and horizontal perspective, not the vertical and gradational one which acknowledges complexity by distinguishing between the average and the above-average, the ordinary and extraordinary.

Awareness of finer distinctions is vital in all current and future efforts to achieve social justice and create a better world; that is, in all protest movements against the globe's rich and powerful and their self-serving policies. This awareness is pivotal because, without it, the protest perspective runs the risk of narrowing into one solely concerned with the satisfying of elementary human needs. If this narrowing were to occur, the perspective would neglect the equally important sphere of human liberties and individuality, where finer distinctions operate.

Among these finer distinctions are the following: Thinking in highly specific terms, as distinct from chiefly collective ones, about the individual; considering what the individual does with the opportunity and wherewithal that has been provided for self-development; recognising the need that pronounced individuality has for distinctive achievement; hoping that the latter is attained, and appraising the individual with reference to this attainment; prizing such attainment as part of a general value placed on social and cultural complexity and diversity.

Neglect of the above considerations might, under certain circumstances, be conscious and deliberate rather than unconscious, indicating an outright hostility to individualism, and for all sorts of reasons linked with the roles of political and social leadership: not least, a dislike of variety and complexity. The need for the protest perspective to be as panoramic as possible, so as to avoid the imposition of uniformity and standardisation, cannot be over-emphasised. In a society without injustice, individuals, in the words of Santayana, "would be born equal, but they would grow unequal, and the only equality subsisting would be equality of opportunity."[e]

In extension of the above points, let's consider the following argument of Raymond Williams (advanced, incidentally, fifty years ago):

> the idea of not a community but an equality of culture—a uniform culture evenly spread—is essentially the product of the primitivism (often expressed as mediaevalism) which was so important a response to the harsh complexities of the new industrial society. Such an idea ignores the *necessary* complexity of any community which employs developed industrial and scientific techniques; and the longing for identity of situation and feeling, which exerts so powerful an emotional appeal in such writers as [William] Morris, is merely a form of regressive longing for a simpler, non-industrial society. In any form of society towards which we are likely to move, it now seems clear that there must be, not a simple equality (in the sense of identity) of culture; but rather a very complex system of specialised developments—the whole of which will form the whole culture, but which will not be available, or conscious as a whole, to any individual or group living within it.[f]

What Williams calls the "necessary complexity" of occupational and cultural pursuits would, as previously said, remain a reality, in an open society, even with the removal of economically dominant groups. Society would go on being multi-faceted, requiring not only many different *kinds* of ability, but also many different *degrees* of ability within these kinds. Thus, even if economic differences (or at least large-scale ones) were to disappear with the departure of group hegemony, differentiation of another type — the capacity type — would continue. This would apply to economic and industrial activity as much as to any other kind, and would be especially pertinent to the economic management of a system designed to meet, adequately and reliably, the material needs of everyone. Across the board, capacity would be an indispensable consideration.

The perspective would be, then, pervasively and inescapably meritocratic. Indeed, it would be more meritocratic than in any previous form of society, since a social structure without the dominance of self-interested groups enjoying special privileges would be one with complete equality of opportunity: therefore one with more space than had ever previously existed for the unhampered display of ability.

Total meritocracy would be precisely the thing to create the enormous cultural complexity which, to paraphrase Williams, no one individual or group could entirely encompass. In so far as meritocracy is justified, there would exist no viable grounds for complaining at that complexity. Nor would there be any justification for the "regressive longing" for some (supposedly) simpler cultural context: a longing which, it must be said, is unfortunately still to be found among some on the Left.

The diversity which meritocracy engenders is at variance with all rigid types of group or 'class' concept. The latter always tend toward oversimplification, and are usually flawed generalisations. Once the individual is viewed as a potential source of initiative and creativity which links him / her with other individuals (whatever their social location) who are capable of similar accomplishments, then rigid group definitions inevitably weaken. To a large extent, this is true even in societies *with* dominant groups (such as present-day Western societies), and would be totally true in a society without them.

End Notes

[a]   *Hamlet*, II 2, ll. 226–7.
[b]   *On Liberty* (Buffalo, New York: Prometheus Bks. Edition, 1986 (1859)), p. 79.
[c]   *Reason in Society* (New York: Dover Publications Inc. edition, 1980 (1905)), p. 101.
[d]   *The Rock*, VIII.
[e]   *Reason in Society*, p. 129.
[f]   *Culture and Society, 1780-1950* (Penguin Bks. Edition, 1963 (1958)), pp. 233–4.

The Relevance of Spengler Today

This essay will focus on Oswald Spengler's most famous work, *The Decline of the West*,[1] published between 1918 and 1922. But first I must specify that I reject the central component of Spengler's argument in this book: that is, the concept of historical necessity, determinism or destiny. According to this concept, the historical process is something which, while operating *through* the actions of human beings, is *not driven by* those actions, and is not dependent for its direction on them. The latter are therefore instrumental to it; it directs human action, not human action it; it is the end to which actions are the means or stepping stones. Thus something called historical necessity is the formative force: something which is more than the mere sequence of human actions, more even than what is disclosed by a point-by-point analysis of the causes and effects of particular actions; something with a shape and structure of its own, informing all the actions which transpire within its framework, and not reducible to them.

The concept of historical determinism, otherwise known as historicism, takes two main forms. One is that the directional impetus is linear, moving in a continuous line. The other is that its is cyclical — with processes in one period being either identical with or equivalent to processes in another period, so that one period either repeats or echoes another. Spengler's position is this cyclical one: specifically the 'equivalence' one. He sees history as unfolding through the life cycles of particular cultures; these, though different from each other, share a common rhythm of development, efflorescence and subsequent decline: a pattern of rise followed by inevitable fall. According to Spengler, Western culture is now in its stage of inescapable decline.[2] As said, I reject historicism in all its forms. This includes the cyclical form.

---

[1] I will in fact be quoting from an abridged version of this text: *The Decline of the West by Oswald Spengler* (hereafter, D.W.O.S.).
[2] This argument, incidentally, made the book enormously appealing to a number of thinkers in the period immediately following World War I, when the repercussions of that conflict were still being keenly felt.

However, such rejection does not leave nothing to commend in Spengler's work. His writing does contain many things of value: a sufficient number, indeed, to lead the eminent historian Sir Arnold Toynbee to speak of Spengler's "brilliant genius".[a] One of these things is what he has to say about the economic and political situation in modern Western society. While I do not accept his argument that Western *culture* is in decline, I do agree with certain aspects of his analysis of the economic and political forces at work in Western society: forces active both when he was writing and now, nearly ninety years later.

In the final part of *Decline*, in the chapters entitled 'Philosophy of Politics' and 'The Machine', he presents a picture in which economic thought is increasingly thought about money — money as an abstract entity — rather than about goods, which are concrete things, and about the concrete social relations involved in the production and exchange of goods by and between peoples and communities. With the increase of money-thought, he argues, economics is becoming more and more impersonal, de-humanised, and insensitive to the grass-roots material activities which actually underpin the economy. Such is the situation in the urban centres of financial speculation, the 'money-markets': the locus in which economic power steadily accumulates, and which increasingly influences the making of major economic decisions.

Spengler's picture — clearly as relevant to 2008 as it was to 1922 — includes further elements which merit serious consideration. He links the growth of a money-economy with that of the power of certain groups of people: industrialists, bankers, financiers and speculators, who form an economic elite exerting massive influence on the political process. This influence corrupts democracy, turning the latter into what is in effect plutodemocracy, where wealth is the main mover and shaker. Thus the machinery of democratic politics becomes an instrument by which the economic objectives of the rich and powerful can be pursued. In this democratic system, the major political parties are subsidized by the very wealthy as a political means by which the latter may attain their *economic* ends. Support given to particular parties may vary, but always that support is determined by economic considerations.

No-one familiar with the workings of the current political system in the world's leading 'democracy', the United States, will be in the least surprised by Spengler's picture. The same point largely applies to a consideration of current 'democracy' in Britain and other advanced industrial economies in the West. Nor will any informed person be shocked by Spengler's characterization of the activities of the most powerful capitalists as "plunderous Vikingism":[b] a phrase echoed in recent times by Ralph Nader and Noam Chomsky when they speak of modern transnational corporations as international kleptocracies.[3]

Spengler, having described with considerable accuracy the modern economic and political realities, goes on to consider what alternative and better situation might emerge. Actually, his considerations take the form of firm predictions, ones made in accordance with his historicist viewpoint, and bound up with another element in that historicism: the notion of Caesarism. Again, without subscribing to his historicism, and also without going into what he means by Caesarism, it is possible to view sympathetically much that he has to say. I personally find his ideas in this area both moving and inspiring; and as applicable, in varying degree, to all progressive forces in the world today who seek to establish genuine democracy and political and economic justice. In reaction to the industrial-financial *status quo*, there will, says Spengler, arise:

> a deep yearning for all old and worthy tradition that still lingers alive. Men are tired to disgust of money-economy. They hope for salvation from somewhere or other, for some true ideal of honour and chivalry, of inward nobility, of unselfishness and duty ... everything that there is of high, money-disdaining ethic ... suddenly becomes the focus of immense life-forces ... The spirit of the knightly orders overpowers plunderous Vikingism ... [this spirit has as its task] the unwearying care for this world as it is, which is the very opposite of the interestedness of the money-power age, and demands high honour and conscientiousness.[c]

While allowance should be made for the rhetorical character of some of Spengler's diction, the basic moral principles espoused in this extract are surely apposite. Their appropriateness is especially clear in view of the chaotic opportunism recently revealed as endemic in the (Western-dominated) global financial system. This opportunism certainly produces the reaction of "disgust" to which Spengler refers.

---

[3] To appreciate the force of this point, one has only to consider the powerful argument now being advanced that the West's major fuel companies are determined to control the production and distribution of oil and gas (the leading industrial fuels) throughout most of south Asia. See this argument's connection with the West's political and military incursions into this area i.e Iraq, the Caspian basin, Afghanistan.

Also, implied in the extract and stated explicitly elsewhere, is a crucial distinction drawn by Spengler between *economic* motivation and that which is *wholly political*. Economic motives belong to industrial-financial elites, but wholly political ones to those who are disinterested and unselfish. The wholly political is "a will to order",[d] an aspiration to achieve genuine social stability and cohesion, and to protect society from selfish groups and elites. Such is the burden of "true rulership, above and beyond all money-advantage": one which stands implacably opposed to "the private powers of the economy" that "want free paths for their acquisition of great resources."[e] Those to whom genuinely political values are the life-blood seek "to call into life a mighty politico-economic order that transcends all class interests, a system of *lofty* thoughtfulness and duty-sense ..."[f]

As is perhaps implied by the above words, Spengler regards the vanguard of action against the present economic system as consisting of a minority of exceptional individuals. He emphatically disagrees with Marx's contention that the key figures in this movement will be a whole social class: the so-called 'working class.' (In fact, throughout *Decline*, his references to Marx are more negative than positive.) Spengler's perspective is akin, among nineteenth century thinkers, to that of Carlyle and Nietzsche,[4] and, among twentieth century figures, to that of Wells, Shaw and Santayana.

Such a perspective, I maintain, remains a very important one. In the previous paragraph, I used the phrase "so-called 'working class'" advisedly. The consensus of a large number of modern sociologists is that there are no clear-cut ways of defining social class. Even if this consensus is rejected, and the term 'working class' is used — as official Marxist theory uses it — to mean everyone who sells his / her labour-power in the labour market (i.e. everyone who is not an employer), then many complex issues still remain. The chief one is the enormous range of differences in ability and skill level, in accomplishment and in moral and intellectual energy, among those who do sell their labour power. These people may all be 'working class' in the sense defined above, but they are still far from being homogenous and unitary.

The same point applies to the more specific social group which many Marxists, in practice as distinct from theory, mean when they

---

[4] Indeed, Nietzsche is described by Spengler as one of the two people (the other being Goethe) "to whom I owe practically everything" (*D.W.O.S.*, p. 20).

speak of the 'working class': those employees who lack advanced qualifications and high-quality abilities and skills. Again, among these a pervasive unity of attributes will be looked for in vain.

Given, then, the difficulties surrounding the use of the term 'working class', it is well to consider alternative perspectives for tackling the problem of economically dominant groups. To insist, as Spengler and others do, that the vanguard and crucial component of the struggle against such dominance will be a morally exceptional minority of individuals, a minority which cannot be defined in class terms, is to present a highly cogent argument. This argument, we should add, is not invalidated by the poorly thought-out charges of 'elitism' and 'snobbism' which are frequently leveled against it. If success in a struggle does, as a matter of fact, require leadership of the highest personal calibre, then this truth should be accepted readily.

Further, sterling leadership is the kind most likely to draw behind it all those people referred to earlier, those who are progressive and committed to social and political justice. These people come from a host of different social and cultural locations; and, for that very reason, will be concerned as much to maintain an open and pluralistic society as to end the hegemony of vested interests.

We see, then, that certain aspects of Spengler's outlook open up a rich vein of thinking, one not accessible to those whose social perspective is, for whatever reason, insufficiently precise. The best in Spengler, as in the words previously quoted, is a reminder of the perennial importance in political life of disinterestedness and of morally outstanding individuals. This point links him not only with the thinkers previously mentioned but also with figures from the ancient world such as Plato and Confucius. Such considerations indicate Spengler's major contribution and on-going relevance to social and political thought.

End Notes

[a] As quoted by Eric Heller in *The Disinherited Mind* (Penguin Bks., 1961 (1952)), p. 162.

[b] D.W.O.S., abridged edition by Helmut Werner (London: George Allen and Unwin Ltd., 1961), p. 377.

[c] *Ibid.*, pp. 376-7.

[d] *Ibid.*, p. 377

[e] For these three quotations, *ibid.*, p. 392.

[f] *Ibid.*, loc. cit.

The 'Princess Casamassima' Problem

The Princess Casamassima is the title of novel by Henry James published in 1886. Set in England, chiefly London, it is a strongly political text portraying the activities of the revolutionary anarchists (pre-Marxist) of the late nineteenth century. But linked to its political themes are broad social and cultural ones. These all converge in the experience of one of the novel's two main characters, Hyacinth Robinson, a highly intelligent young man from an under-privileged background who is taken up by an Italian aristocratic lady living in England and interested in revolutionary politics—the lady whose name gives the book its title.

What, then, is the 'problem' the novel deals with? A multi-themed text such as this deals with many issues, but the one I will focus on is perhaps the most challenging one: the difficulty of reconciling democratic egalitarianism with the attitude which places high value on cultural achievements arising from social and economic conditions which are distinctly *in*egalitarian. Here, the egalitarian view in question is that everyone should be equal in condition, economic and cultural. This position is best represented in the novel by the anarchist Hoffendahl, who also, significantly, shows a complete failure to appreciate the great art of the past. Against this position, James sets an alternative perspective, one which Hyacinth comes to see with increasing clarity: that, in the words of critic Walter Allen, "the creation of certain kinds of art and styles of living, generally regarded as good in themselves, and the establishment of democratic values, may be mutually exclusive, for each may exist only at the expense of the other."[a]

In partial support of the above, it can be argued that, economically, complete equality of condition would preclude the development of certain kinds of art and life-style which require extensive material resources. Clearly, as matters now stand socially, and as they have stood in the past, it is only in exceptionally fortunate conditions that such projects can be pursued extensively; and these conditions, by definition, cannot be the norm. Thus *in*equality of condition is a prerequisite for cultural achievements which need large-scale material resourcing and which are, at the same time, distinctive and valuable in themselves.

These observations are, essentially, as true of present-day society as they were of James's. While it is the case that, in the West at any rate, general living standards are much higher than in James's day, still material resources remain finite. Also, though they could be much more evenly distributed, that distribution would, as said, block those kinds of cultural development requiring material inequality. If no one individual or group possessed much larger economic assets than any other, then all cultural projects would have to be very limited, economically, in scale. Large scale cultural achievements are, in the novel, specified by Hyacinth in a letter to the Princess: "The monuments and treasures of art, the great palaces and properties…the general fabric of civilization as we know it …"[b] What Hyacinth is talking about will be obvious to any discerning person who knows what major cities such as London, Paris or Rome have to offer culturally—especially architecturally. Westminster, Versailles and the Vatican are among instances that spring to mind.

Material inequality, then, remains indispensable for certain kinds of culture. With this in mind, I wish to briefly examine the cultural implications of the view—basically socialist or social democratic—that economic equality or near-equality is the general social condition to be aimed at. On this view, it can be cogently argued that, in modern society, the state, with its enormous financial resources, should be the agency to replace private wealth as provider of large-scale cultural products. If this were to happen, inequality of condition would continue, but *not within* society, only between it and the body politic, and then with society's consent.

There are merits in this argument, but also problems. One difficulty is that government might be tempted to use artistic projects as propaganda tools. This is always a danger when the body-politic subscribes to a rigid ideology: a danger that was graphically illustrated by the policies of the totalitarian regimes of Hitler, Stalin and Mussolini in the twentieth century.

At the opposite end of the spectrum, a very different kind of problem is to do with the position the state occupies in a genuinely open and pluralistic society of the type which has been, to a large extent, achieved in the West. The questions arise: Which of the many cultural outlooks would government respond to sympathetically? Which criteria would its funding choices be based on? (In this regard, it should be remembered that governments in modern democratic societies do not have the automatic cultural authority and certainty they possessed in pre-democratic societies, where they shared a clearly delineated cultural outlook—usually including a strong religious element— with the landed aristocracy from which they were mostly derived.) Further, there is the consideration that the state would have to depend on people outside its own ranks for artistic ability. Since an open society is one in which no single cultural form enjoys hegemony, the questions of which artistic styles the state would favour, and how it would judge the calibre of individual artists, would not be easy ones to answer.

The above line of thinking obviously opens up a wide range of ideas regarding the cultural aspects of an economically egalitarian society. It actually takes us beyond that found in James's novel, for the simple reason that it refers to social developments which have occurred in the 120 years since the book was published. In the West at least, we can speak, as James and his contemporaries could not, from experience of a society which is extensively open and fluid in the educational and cultural senses, and to a lesser extent in the economic sense: a society in which an unprecedented range of cultural achievements is available for the general population to access.

At the same time, as we have seen, difficult questions remain concerning cultural attainments of the large-scale and spectacular kind: those to which the word 'grandeur' can be applied. If present Western society seeks grandeur—as in fact all societies of an advanced kind have done—then it should do so only in ways which are compatible with its open and democratic character. Hence grandeur in the modern context must not co-exist with gross social and economic inequities: the kind which were present in James's day and, indeed, in almost all advanced societies known to history. If the socialist / social democratic argument is accepted, then the only economic inequality which should legitimately obtain is that between society as a whole and the body politic, with the former freely granting to the latter the enormous cultural resources which were previously the province of private citizens or non-democratic governments, or both. If, on the other hand, economic egalitarianism is rejected as a social model, then—given the general social progress which has been made since James's day—ways must be found to combine the pursuit of cultural grandeur by private citizens[1] with the avoidance of extreme and rigid differences in economic, social and cultural opportunity. As part of this, there must be no social groups who are

---

[1] A pursuit that could perhaps be subsidised by government.

in any sense submerged. While the government is not asked to do what private citizens can do, what the latter do should be accessible to all.

End Notes

[a] In *The English Novel* (London: Pheonix House Ltd., 1960 (1954)), p. 261.
[b] As quoted by Allen, *ibid.*, p. 260.

Multi – Culturalism in English Society
Some Advantages and Problems

First, some of the advantages: By and large, and despite the activities of far-Right organisations such as the British National Party, the increasing presence of different cultural and ethnic groups in England from the 1960s onwards has genuinely widened the outlook of most white Anglo-Saxons. They have become more understanding of and sympathetic to cultural variety — more internationally-minded than they generally were up to the 60s.

Anyone whose childhood was, like mine, spent in the 1950s will recognise in retrospect the conspicuous cultural insularity of English life at that time: a time when, it should be remembered, England still possessed some part of its empire. At a popular cultural level, the chief external influence continued to be American culture. But, with the exception of the impact on young people of rock-and-roll music, this influence remained largely what it had been in the period up to World War II: mainly cinema, and popular music whose heyday had been in the inter-war years. Also, the influence was limited: not enough to reduce, to any significant degree, the distinctive 'Englishness' of the way of life.[1]

The growth in responsiveness to a wide range of other cultures coincided, significantly, with the final stages of England's decline as an imperial power. One of the problems about the mentality which was widespread in the 1950s, and across all social classes, was the illusion that England was still a world power on the scale it had been before World War II. This illusion was evident in much of the foreign policy of that decade, with rear-guard colonial wars being fought in Kenya and Malaya, and at a time when India had already been lost and other colonies such as Nigeria and Ghana were about to be lost.

---

[1] There are of course many sources which can be consulted for evidence of this 'Englishness'. One of the best remains George Orwell's essay 'England, Your England', published in 1940 but still highly relevant for most of the 1950s.

At the cultural level, the illusion was also manifest, though to lesser degree, in the many war films made during this period. While it can be argued that these films expressed a justifiable sense of pride in depicting victory over Nazism, two further points need to be borne in mind. Firstly, this pride in past achievements could be seen as, to some extent, a bulwark against full awareness of reduced status in the post-war world. Secondly, these films, in their presentation of the officer-class and the ranks, clearly endorsed the rigid divisions in English society which had obtained in the pre-war world, when England had in fact been the leading world power. Hence such endorsement could be viewed as a further way of perpetuating the illusion under discussion. In other words, there was linkage between national pride and acceptance of the traditional social structure.

This linkage is all the more worthy of attention in view of the fact that the traditional social structure still persisted, to a large extent, in the England of the 1950s. This was despite the establishment of the Welfare State from 1945–51, and the expansion of educational opportunity: an expansion which, in terms of higher education, did not really become radical until the 1960s. Given the large measure of continuity in social conditions, it was not surprising that many people from lower income and occupational groups shared the uncritical nationalism of the more affluent and powerful groups.

It would of course be wrong to say that, in later decades, uncritical nationalism sank without trace. It is always strong among certain social groups, especially fascists. Also, arguably we have seen a resurgence of it with the militaristic foreign policy of the New Labour government over the last eight years. However, it was definitely the case that such nationalism went into comparative decline in the 1960s. This was, indeed, a period when a large section of English society as a whole underwent something of an identity crisis: it suffered a loss of the self-confidence and resilience which its parents had shown in the war years and the immediate post-war period. It was acutely aware of diminished status internationally, and the last remnants of empire had now gone. Also, customary faith in many political and social institutions was wavering. Overall, for many thinking people, this was a period of immense uncertainty, anxiety and lack of direction.

At the same time, such a painful experience of doubt, re-appraisal and revision was a necessary condition for the change to a more receptive outlook on the world that was unquestionably needed.

Gradually, that change came, increasingly prompted by the growing multi-culturalisation of the country from, as said, the 60s onwards. The growth of a cosmopolitan perspective was only to some extent impeded by the political phenomenon of Thatcherism in the 1980s and early 90s — by, that is, a mentality which in many ways tried to resurrect the social atmosphere of the 1950s, and, indeed, of earlier periods.[2] 'Only to some extent', to repeat, since by this time even the most die-hard Conservatives had to accept and publicly acknowledge that England was a multi-cultural society; and such acknowledgement has continued among Conservatives (regardless of whether or not they actually approve of the social fact). The general acceptance of multi-culturalism over the last fifty years has meant that there has been no return to the scale of nationalistic thinking and cultural insularity which existed, as said, in the 1950s and earlier.[3]

One of the many advantages of multi-culturalism in England has been a much increased appreciation of the cultures of the Indian sub-continent: an area which had been one of England's earliest and largest colonies, and one which was, arguably, the most complex culturally. Up until not so long ago, very few English people had much appreciation of that complexity.[4] While the extent of appreciation varies widely, from enjoyment of high-quality cuisine[5] to absorption in Indian philosophical and religious doctrines, there is simply much more of it than there was fifty years ago.

Moreover, sub-continent culture plays a major role in the many multi-cultural festivals which now frequently take place, and which are both well publicised and well attended. Perhaps the best known of these is the Notting Hill carnival, an annual London event held in

---

[2] Significantly, Thatcherism made many disparaging references to the society of the 1960s.
[3] There are current arguments for 'Englishness' (and for 'Britishness'), but they do not have the same force as the nationalistic feeling of the 50s. At that time, many nationalists did not think that reasoned argument was required at all. Also, we should note that in the 50s racism was unashamedly blatant, and not just on the part of politically far-Right groups. In addition to things like the Notting Hill riots in London, there was overt discrimination in private-sector housing — discrimination which met with little legal redress.
[4] A notable exception was the writer E.M. Forster, whose novel about an Englishman's experience of India, *A Passage to India*, remains a very illuminating text, even though it was published as long ago as 1924.
[5] A phenomenon not, incidentally, to be under-estimated. The impact of Indian food on eating-out habits in England, habits which are culturally and socially significant, has been considerable. The same is true of Chinese and other Asian cuisines. Partly because of the wide availability of these cuisines, more English people eat out than they did before the 1960s.

the very same area which was, in the 50s, the scene of bitter race riots. This fact is indeed an index of how times have changed. In the 50s, multi-cultural festivals were almost non-existent: the integrative social experience which produces them was simply not there. Also, outside of the white, Anglo-Saxon majority, the racial and ethnic minorities — chiefly Jews and Italians — were quite small and generally not given to public cultural display.

In the above and other ways, English cultural life is now more cosmopolitan, colourful and multifarious than it has probably ever been. Major gains have been made in knowledge, responsiveness and sensitivity. England, or at least urban England, is now very much part of what is figuratively called the global village.

However, there have been problems as well. The first of these is connected with aspects of English culture which are also aspects of certain other cultures: ones which are scientifically advanced.

A scientifically advanced culture is one that has adopted scientific method as either the main or the only means of gaining objective knowledge. While having a critically alert attitude toward scientific procedure, it nevertheless regards the latter as being the most reliable means for discovering how reality is structured. With its reliance on science, such a culture is an open one in every intellectual sense: as in all genuine scientific activity, it is constantly prepared to question, revise or amend established viewpoints; hence it is non-dogmatic. Also, it is prepared to sustain the burdens which such open-mindedness brings with it: the problems and anxieties caused by the absence of absolute or final certainties.

English culture since the sevenenteenth century, and especially since the nineteenth century, has increasingly become a scientifically advanced one. Such, at least, has been the achievement of many of its most prominent intellects. This has been the case despite — in the political sphere — the imperialistic character of English foreign policy from the eighteenth century to the mid twentieth; and despite the continuance of social injustice within English society during this period: the rigidity of class divisions, and inequality of educational, cultural and economic opportunity. A further negative factor during this period was the persistence, in society as a whole, of non-scientific ways of thinking. Yet, these factors notwithstanding, English culture at its best, over the last three centuries, has been in the vanguard of intellectual modernity.

This is a distinction which it of course shares with certain other cultures: in the Western context, those of France, Germany and the

United States are obvious examples. Again, in these countries, scientific advance has unfortunately co-existed with a large measure of social injustice and with non-scientific modes of thought. Further, outside the Western context, there are other cultures which are also part of intellectual modernity, while having various kinds of social drawbacks.

For all such cultures, a fundamental problem arises when they come into contact with ones in which a religious mindset is dominant or predominant. A religious mindset is one which does not regard scientific method as the main or only means of discovering the structure of reality. It is one which, on the contrary, views faith and revelation as, if not the only, then the ultimate way of making such discovery. Usually, this means belief in deity as the final and fullest source of knowledge.

Returning to the English context: the process of multi-culturalisation has, to a significant degree, brought conflict between scientific culture and that which is ultimately non-scientific. A chief example of the latter is Islamic fundamentalism, which in recent years has challenged the values associated with scientific culture and free thought more vehemently than has any other religious group, emphatically more than the Anglican Church, England's most influential ecclesiastical body,[6] and more than other Protestant sects, as well as more than Catholicism and Judaism. The Islamic example highlights a general problem: tension will inevitably arise between a culture long reared in scientific thinking and one (be it, in fact, religious or not) which lacks an adequate scientific background, which refuses to open itself up to science to any significant extent, and which refuses social compromise of any kind. Mainly because of Islamic fundamentalism, such tension now exists in English society, on a scale not seen for a very long time.

It should be added, however, that another, lesser factor contributing to the tension is strictly of home growth: far-Right racism and fascism, with its pseudo-scientific arguments about racial and even national superiority.

Now for the second problem. It is to do with level of linguistic appreciation. In any literate culture which has a long and complex history, the main language develops in range and power of expression to reach a high point, or a series of high points. This may hap-

---

[6] It should be remembered that Anglicanism has constantly had to modify its doctrines over the last 150 years, precisely because of the continuous scientific advances made in its home country during this period.

pen, incidentally, even if the culture is not scientifically advanced, or is completely pre-scientific. For example, people who regard Shakespeare's usage as the most eloquent and expressive level which English has so far reached will therefore argue that this zenith was attained in a largely pre-scientific culture, as indeed English culture was in Shakespeare's day: a culture prior to the emergence of modern science in the seventeenth century. Anyway, whatever the type of culture in which linguistic excellence appears, the fact of excellence is the point to be focussed on. With English, many people vote Shakespeare as the high point; with Italian, many cite Dante; with French, Voltaire is the frequent choice; with German, many opt for Goethe; with Greek, Plato is often first choice. Whether one endorses these verdicts or not, the key consideration is clearly that language can be raised to great heights, ones which will not easily be equalled or surpassed.

The historical fact is that elevation of language usage develops from the prolonged and sustained progress of *one* language in an environment which is sufficiently integrated to facilitate such progress. In other words, a high degree of social and cultural *homogeneity* is indispensable. People need to share a large number of experiences within a main cultural framework, and they also need to articulate their responses to those experiences within a main linguistic framework. That this kind of focus and concentration is an essential factor in the development of a language is shown by study of the evolution of English, French, German and Italian, and of all languages which have reached extraordinary heights.

However, in an environment which is increasingly multi-cultural, no one language can firmly hold a privileged position and be given much more room to develop than any other. Now, returning to the English context: if the votaries of Shakespeare are correct, or even if those of some other great author of the past are,[7] we are looking at a linguistic situation in which, by common agreement, summits have already been reached, and were reached long before the large-scale advent of multi-culturalism. As regards English, then, the canon of excellence is well established and secure: so far, so good. But questions arise about the future situation, educationally and in other respects, in a multi-cultural context.

Firstly, how many people whose first or main language is not English will ever gain any substantial appreciation of the heights the language has scaled? Unless they study English in an extensively

---

[7]   For example, Milton, Pope, Dickens or James.

academic way, they surely will not. This question has all the more force when one sees that it also applies to many white Anglo-Saxons, whose first language *is* English but who, for social, economic or cultural reasons, never reach an appreciation of the language's finest achievements. (This situation is of course not just a present-day problem likely to be projected into the future. It has existed for a very long time: a fact which partly suggests the inadequacy of the national education system). Since, in the contemporary urban context, both categories of people — especially young people — increasingly mix together, it is likely that ignorance of English's full linguistic character and potential will continue. Those whose first language is English will have no deep linguistic knowledge, either to benefit from themselves or to convey to those whose first language is not English. So, in this context, traditional English will not expand in use and reach further levels of articulateness. It is true that, in this same context, sub-cultural forms of English do develop, as a common argot between groups with different language backgrounds, but these forms are of course a far cry from traditional usage, and are unlikely ever to match the latter in complexity.

It is the case that a full appreciation of English, as a regular feature of cultural awareness, will persist among certain social groups — the highly educated and widely informed; and these do and will continue to include some people whose first language is not English. However, these are a minority of the population. The hope of course is that this minority will eventually become the majority, but such a development is improbable. More likely, they will remain peripheral, and so will not occupy the social centre-ground. The latter's occupants will be, then, people — from underprivileged backgrounds but also from other social areas as well — who have little or no historical or aesthetic interest in English, and who mix with other ethnic groups which also, by and large, lack this interest. If society becomes even more multi-cultural and multi-lingual, concern for the historical and aesthetic aspects of English is likely to be even further eclipsed. Given the increasing linguistic variety that surrounds them, the majority of people will be even less inclined than they are now to develop an interest in, or draw attention to, those features of the language.

As with a sense of linguistic continuity, so with a sense of historical continuity: a third problem associated with multi-culturalism is the weakening of appreciation of a country's indigenous historical heritage. This point, I should hasten to add, is made not from an attitude of partisan nationalism, but from the recognition that English history, like that of so many other countries, is uniquely complex. It is, of course, a mixture of positive and negative elements, like that of all nations, but still it constitutes a corpus of facts of tremendous interest and intricacy. Particular attention should be given to the long struggle between monarchical power and other social groups: a struggle which paved the way for the West's first kind of formally representative government since that of ancient Athens, and hence for the beginnings of modern democratic politics — an initiative which was later to resound decisively throughout the Western world and then the whole world. English history certainly merits protracted study; and, while such study may not be, for a range of reasons, possible for everyone, it remains *intrinsically* worthwhile.

This of course is not to say that English history should be given sole attention; it needs to be studied in relation to the histories of other countries, particularly European ones. But it is to say that, for English people, it should be the main interest because it is bound up with what they *know best*: a daily life informed by a specific social inheritance and set of traditions — things to which the daily round offers frequent conduits. Because connected with the social conditions that are known best, their national history is the kind people should strive to know best.

However, the more multi-cultural England becomes, the less inducement will there probably be for the majority of people to sustain a focus of interest on England's past. The many-coloured ethnic variety of the present creates so many alternative directions of interest; and for those with an orientation toward history, that of the countries from which England's ethnic minorities originated can, quite understandably, become a focus of attention. Such interest is of course legitimate and important, but, again, it does deflect from what can be known best.

Santayana once said that one's eyes should survey the world, but one's feet should be planted in one's own country. These words best summarise the above argument in favour of a concentration of historical interest.

In general conclusion: living in a multi-cultural society involves many benefits but is also a matter of striving to create a delicate balance, which is no easy task. The balance is between openness to the new and concern for the old; between responsiveness to what is unfamiliar and a valuing of what is familiar and traditional. In connection with the latter, the national past and its heritage must be viewed critically and without illusions, if what is genuinely valuable in them is to be recognised; and there is much that is genuinely valuable. While it is important to possess all kinds of knowledge, knowledge of the most focussed and concentrated kind is the most illuminating; hence, even in the midst of a vibrant cultural plurality, a main cultural commitment is always needed. In English society, as in others like it, that main commitment should include an engagement with science, the national language and the national history. To an engagement with all three spheres, an increasing multi-culturalism poses, or will probably pose, various types of problem. The latter are, actually or potentially, extensive, and therefore require sustained consideration.

Political Revolutions in Complex Cultures

A complex culture can be defined in a number of inter-related ways. Some are as follows:
- a) Most obviously, a culture with writing
- b) One in which individuality has achieved major status, as distinct from one in which it is of little importance. Hence such a culture is found in societies which are, in the words of the classic sociologist Emile Durkheim, 'organic' rather than 'mechanical'.
- c) A culture which, while being in an organic context, is also in one which possesses a high level of social organisation and order.
- d) One which is always open to new ways of thinking, and especially those ways bound up with empiricism and scientific method. This culture is a feature of societies which are, in the words of Karl Popper, 'open' and not 'closed'.
- e) A culture which has a strongly developed sense of history and historical heritage, plus extensive historical data at its disposal.
- f) One which clearly distinguishes between human necessities (what is necessary for a basic level of human wellbeing) and human liberties (what people should be free to achieve once the basic level of wellbeing has been attained)
- g) A culture which has an hierarchical and even canonical sense of achievement and accomplishment, as part of the respect it accords to individuality and also to group attainment.
- h) One which possesses and welcomes wide diversity in human groupings and orientations: occupationally, artistically, and in other ways.

Given these eight criteria, it might be replied that what is being defined here is only one form of complex culture—the liberal-individualist form, as it has emerged in the West over the last two hundred years or so. What about, it might be asked, the complex cultures of the ancient world, especially of Egypt and Mesopotamia; and what of the European Middle Ages, and traditional oriental cultures such as those of China and India? In these, respect for individuality was nowhere near as widespread as it is in the context of modern Western liberalism; nor was there anything like the openness to new ways of thinking found in this context. True: but at the same time, these cultures did, within limits, meet other criteria in the list. They had a strong sense of what they at least regarded as history, possessing chronicles and genealogies even if they did not engage in the complex historiography which is now viewed as genuine historical study. Also, among privileged minorities in these societies, there was diversity and variety of activity and achievement. There existed, in addition, an hierarchical sense of attainment, especially the aspiration to artistic grandeur—as shown by, for example, the seven 'wonders' of the ancient world and the mediaeval cathedrals. Finally, they were all accompanied by high levels of social organisation.

Clearly, not all complex cultures meet all eight criteria, but all meet some. Equally clearly, we are touching here on massively intricate historical issues. We must therefore limit our sphere of reference if we are to have a working concept of what a complex culture is, a concept to which we can then apply political considerations.

These considerations focus on the idea of revolution. The latter, in its extreme form, can be defined as the attempt at complete overthrowal of the political, social, economic and cultural *status quo;* as distinct from the reform, amendment or modification of the latter. Given this characterisation, the question that emerges is: can a very complex *status quo* ever be fully done away with? Related questions are: does its complexity reflect at least some basic tendencies in human behaviour; and, if so, can these tendencies ever be fully eradicated? Obviously, these questions do not arise in the case of simple cultural formations, ones which are inevitably superseded in the event of a widening of outlets for human capacities to express themselves.

In cultures which meet most or all of the eight criteria previously listed, the cultural fabric is rich because of gradual growth. Hence the sense of history and tradition is very strong, and so, as a result, is the sense of certain basic similarities between present and past behaviour. From this arises the view that there are important lessons to be learned from the past. Further, this view can be held without the belief that past and present are exactly the same.

An outlook which is keenly aware of linkage between what is happening now and what has happened previously is unlikely to accept the extreme revolutionary argument that a total metamorphosis in human behaviour, a root-and-branch transformation of it, is possible—let alone possible in a short space of time as a consequence of a series of political actions. If such a transformation did occur, it would mean that all the major cultural achievements of the past, especially in literature, could no longer produce a deeply sympathetic response—only a distanced and critical one, registered by a 'new' humanity toward the 'old' humanity.[1] In any complex culture where freedom of thought obtains to a large extent, as it does in present Western society, such a situation is hard to imagine. This is so despite all the changes which have taken place over the centuries in the society in which the culture is located. Thus the extreme revolutionary argument, as distinct from the moderate revolutionary one or the evolutionary and reformist one, has its work cut out in convincing people that a total, as distinct from partial, break with the past can be made.

Its job is especially hard in the light of the totalitarian and repressive consequences of the two major political revolutions of the twentieth century: that in Russia in 1917 (see footnote 1) and China in 1949. These consequences showed that tyranny had not become a thing of the past, and that enormous dangers attend a radicalism which is bound up with ideological extremism.

If we date modern political revolution from 1789, and if we take the French Revolution of that year and the Russian Revolution of 1917 as the two key moments in modern revolutionism, we see that each went through a moderate, then extremist phase. In France, the moderates were the Girondins, and the extremists the Jacobins. In Russia, the moderates were the Mensheviks, and the extremists the Bolsheviks. That in each case there was initially a period of moderation partly reflects the fact that French society and culture before 1789, and Russian before 1917, were, in their different ways, highly

---

[1] It is true that this attitude was displayed by several people in post-revolutionary Russia: people under strong ideological influence. But the attitude was not the product of genuine freedom of thought, nor held by everyone, nor long-lasting.

complex.[2] This complexity existed despite the repressiveness of the political regimes in each country. Moderates acknowledge complexity, especially that of historical heritage. They are of the view that human development does not proceed in sudden jumps, that the past cannot simply be dispensed with, and that elements and reverberations of it continue meaningfully into the present. This kind of outlook did obtain in France, and to a lesser extent in Russia, when moderates were in control, before giving way to extremism.[3]

As I have argued in a previous essay, 'The Protest Perspective and Meritocracy', a major and justifiable reason for rebelling against the *status quo* is inequality of opportunity: social, economic, cultural. Such rebellion does not involve complete rejection of the present or past order of things, since what is being challenged is deprivation of opportunity for full participation in these things. This is especially so in the cultural sphere. Hence political revolutionaries who think positively only or mainly about a future social order show their ignorance of the fact that much discontent is bound up with valuing what the present and past have to offer: with, in other words, being denied adequate access to what is currently valued. This situation is inevitable in a complex culture.

Complexity means continuity, development over long periods of time, striking deep roots, laying durable foundations. As such, it provides the basis for great art and philosophy and other kinds of

[2] As regards France: in the eighteenth century, its intellectual culture was, arguably, the leading one in Europe. Voltaire, Rousseau, Diderot, D'Alembert, D'Holbach, Condorcet and others: certainly no other European country at this time surpassed France in quantity of major thinkers. Also, though a good deal of the thinking was connected with protest against the *ancien regime*, much of it was on other subjects, of a general philosophical nature, with a relevance extending far beyond the political context in which it was produced.
  As regards Russia: the nineteenth century was the greatest period in Russian literature. Tolstoy, Dostoyevsky, Turgenev, Gogol, Pushkin, and (latterly) Chekhov: this roll-call had no equal in Russia before, and has had none since. Further, the Russian achievement in fiction is unquestionably on a par with that of the two other major European centres of novel writing in the nineteenth century, England and France. More specifically, Tolstoy's *War and Peace* is widely regarded as the greatest novel ever written (with other work by Tolstoy and novels by Dostoyevsky ranking very high in this listing). As with France in the eighteenth century, much of the material was not to do with political protest, and dealt with themes transcending the political context in which it was written.
[3] The extremism in turn eventually led to the emergence of autocrats: men who were more hard-headed pragmatists and opportunists than ideologues — Napoleon in France, Stalin in Russia.

intellectual achievement which emerge from prolonged consideration of large areas of human experience, gathered within the framework of relative social stability. This stability is essential for fashioning a long-range view. Thus long-range perspectives cannot be formed during periods of intense upheaval and revolution, which is why very little major art appears during these periods. It is of course no valid *political* criticism of revolutionary periods to note that they are not artistically momentous, but the observation does return us to our main point about the position occupied by revolutions in the larger context.

For the above reasons, revolutions are not important parts of cultural history; and even if they precede, even pave the way for, periods which are, this is partly because the subsequent periods re-absorb a good deal of the important culture which existed before the revolution. This can happen even when the revolution seeks to separate itself from the cultural complexity which preceded it by becoming extremely repressive and creating social conditions which are crude and even atavistic. Cultural re-absorption was what happened in France in the nineteenth century, from 1815 onward. Despite the many political problems faced by French society in this period, the culture did regain much of the intellectual richness which had characterised the eighteenth century: a richness that had been impossible during the Jacobin phase of the Revolution and the subsequent rule of Napoleon.

Staying for a moment on the subject of French culture, it is worth noting that Marcel Proust, one of the greatest of twentieth century novelists, spoke of[a] major French writers who had lived long before the Revolution but who remain great even though they knew nothing of that event. This observation reinforces what has previously been said about the distinction to be drawn between cultural achievement and political upheaval. Proust speaks from within his own country's cultural perspective, but of course a large number of other national perspectives and authors can be invoked: Sophocles, Dante, Shakespeare and Cervantes are among many figures of perennial importance who pre-date, by wide margins, the year 1789. The implication is that profound insights are not granted to a writer because he lives in a particular political context or era. Those insights are granted because s/he is both intrinsically great and lives in a period which can bring out that greatness. Many different sorts of period can do this. This is of course not to deny that the outlooks of great minds are, in varying degree, dependent on historical circumstances; as said, innate greatness needs external stimulus. But it is to assert that this dependence is not total, that greatness involves the ability to transcend the social conditions which first stimulated it.

Finally, focussing briefly on contemporary Western society, it is true to say that, among the most discerning, an attitude of moderation now prevails in approaches to political issues. This attitude is perhaps best encapsulated by Popper in *The Open Society and Its Enemies*, first published in 1945, at the end of World War II and of a roughly thirty-year period of massive violence, political upheaval and intense ideological conflict in Europe. Such turmoil had been the enemy of cultural depth and continuity, largely because ideological extremism (of both political Right and Left) had, as always, denied complexity. Extremism is always over-ambitious in its political projects. In reaction to this whole way of thinking, Popper argued for modest, piecemeal efforts at social reform, ones which were oriented to specific issues and evils and which did not attempt any sweeping, across-the-board and utopianist programmes for social transformation: efforts which were, then, not revolutionary in any extremist sense but gradualist, *ad hoc* and meliorist; and all imbued with the spirit of intellectual openness and flexibility.

Though perhaps the best known advocate of the above position, Popper was by no means alone in arguing for it in the immediate post-war period. It is also found in Albert Camus's *The Rebel* (1951), a text whose key word is "le mesure" (moderation); and in a good deal of Bertrand Russell's social and political writing during this period. Other authors such as E.M. Forster and Isaiah Berlin should also be mentioned in this regard.

Thus the contemporary champion of moderation, flexibility and critical acuteness has a strong heritage to draw on, and should feel no discomfort in so doing. This heritage is certainly needed at the present time, which has seen a resurgence of vehemently fundamentalist styles of thinking of various kinds. Again, for the most discerning, not this latter mindset but one based on knowledge, investigation, critical acumen, examination of assumptions and overcoming of prejudices is affirmed as the way ahead.

Such an outlook, free as it is of all kinds of political correctness, may well find itself tending toward a culturally hierarchical viewpoint: one which values the great achievements of the past as much as it does those of the present—indeed, which understands that present greatness is intelligible chiefly with reference to past greatness. The hierarchical perspective has in fact already gained a lot of ground in recent years, in vigorous opposition to the arguments of cultural relativists; one of its most notable spokespeople being the eminent literary critic Harold Bloom.[4]

The hierarchist, for example in English-language culture, feels no embarrassment about arguing for the permanent value of writers such as Shakespeare, Dickens and Jane Austen. This is the case despite the many social changes which took place in England between the sixteenth and nineteenth centuries, and the many which have transpired since the nineteenth. Also, the hierarchist finds support in what is happening at the level of popular media, with stagings of Shakespeare's plays probably as numerous as they have been at any time since the eighteenth, and with film and TV adaptations of Shakespeare, Dickens and Austen both frequent and influential.

Hierarchism weds present to past. In so doing, it constitutes a very important part of the balanced, informed and moderate outlook which all complex cultures require, but which is no part of the ideological extremism that attempts to carry political change, and change of other kinds, to immoderate lengths.

End Note

[a] In Volume 12 of his chief work, *Remembrance of Things Past*.

---

[4] See in particular Bloom's *The Western Canon* and *Shakespeare and the Invention of the Human*.

Determinism and Prescription

Reproduced, with amendments, with kind permission of the Editor of *The Ethical Record*.

> because every act of man's will, and every desire, and every inclination proceedeth from some cause, and that from another cause in a continuall chaine ... they proceed from *necessity*. So that to him that could see the connexion of those causes, the *necessity* of all men's voluntary actions would appear manifest.
>
> *Thomas Hobbes*[a]

Let's begin by defining what is meant by 'cause': it is an event which compels the incidence of a specific subsequent event.

The deterministic thesis of continuous causation amounts to the view that every human action, no matter how momentous, is part of a mechanism constituting the total activity of the agent. Since constant causation does obtain, every human action is an effect as well as a cause, a link in an unbroken chain, a component of a mechanistic continuum. This being the case, is reference to action bound to be nothing more than description / explanation: a statement of causal linkage, and therefore only of fact, of what *is*? Can it, then, never be a statement of what *ought to be* i.e. prescription, as distinct from description?

Indeed, does determinism place the very act of prescribing, completely and inescapably, within its descriptive framework, seeing it as just another link in a mechanistic sequence? Hence is there no space at all in determinism for discourse and argumentation of a prescriptive kind, as opposed to mere causal analysis of prescriptive acts? Is there, then, no going beyond the descriptive process, no way of breaking out of it into a sphere of advocacy and exhortation which is autonomous of cause, and which in turn appeals to autonomy in its hearers?

In considering these questions, we should begin by noting that many determinists accept Hume's argument that the regularities of event-sequence which we observe in nature are not in themselves proof that causality exists. According to this argument, causality, and therefore causal laws, are our interpretations of regular sequence, constructions we place on it. These interpretations are certainly very reasonable ones — arguably the most reasonable possible; but interpretations they remain.

Further, most determinists concede that the postulate of universal causation, in addition to being a construction, is a working hypothesis only. They accept the prevalent view in modern physics that what are called causal laws are, in relation to the future, probabilistic only. Thus the regularities which occurred in the past and continue in the present will, not certainly but only probably, recur in the future.

These modifications of the argument for determinism are important to acknowledge. Nevertheless, determinists continue to regard their position as — to repeat — a working hypothesis, one on which they actively base prediction and action. Hence we return to the core issue of mechanism: the assumption, albeit provisional and non-dogmatic, of an unbroken continuity of cause and effect; and to the relation between this assumption and the question of prescriptive discourse.

Given the centrality of this assumption, the view of the morally-concerned determinist logically has to be that prescription *does* have a place within a causalist framework, and that it *is* compatible with causal explanation. In other words, prescription is morally valid even though it has causes, and even though its impact on its audience is also caused. Its validity can be argued for from an intentionalist standpoint: in terms of the morally approvable effects which the prescription intends. The intentionalist argument clearly focuses on the intrinsic character of the prescriptive act, the distinctive status it possesses within the causal framework. To possess this status, the act does not, and does not need to, separate itself from the mechanistic continuum. Being an effect in no way demeans it.

It will be seen that a key feature of this position is its rejection of a traditionally held view in moral philosophy (associated especially with Judaeo-Christian thought) that an act can be moral only if it is uncaused and therefore the expression of an absolute and unconditioned free will.

To focus on the intrinsic status of an act as a component of a causal sequence is to argue that no prior factor can bestow that status. In other words, the act is not given its character by its cause. That character is constituted by the act itself. In this sense, cause remains extrinsic to the act, while at the same time being, of course, its *sine qua non*. Effect has one identity, cause another.

The argument that moral prescription is not invalidated by the facts that it is caused and that it intends to serve as a cause carries a very important implication: that issues of justification—central to ethical discourse—do not dissolve into issues of explanation. To explain why justification is sought is not to invalidate such seeking. We are back to the point about the intrinsic character of something which is an effect. In ethical discourse, actions always stand in need of justification, no matter how deterministic the premises underlying the discourse.

This means that questions of moral justification, prescription and recommendation, while anchored to causal considerations, extend upward—so to speak—into a region of their own. Hence they give to ethical discourse a unique dimension, one additional to the purely factual dimension constituted by causal considerations.

End Note

[a]   *Leviathan* (London and New York: Everyman's Library, 1970 (1651)), p. 111.

Compatibilist Freedom and Global Causation

Compatibilism is the doctrine that a person enjoys freedom when he does what he wants to do, and is not prevented from such action by any impediment or coercion external to himself. At the same time, this freedom is not separate from causality: when a person does what he wants to do, he acts as a result of his internal desires and aspirations, and the latter themselves are the result of prior factors. Hence, freedom is compatible with causality—when the causality is completely internal, and has nothing to do with extraneous compulsion, restriction or constriction.

This kind of freedom is, manifestly, of a relative and not absolute character. Absolute freedom would mean the absence of causation of any kind, and is the type postulated by libertarians. By contrast, relative freedom does involve causation, of the kind stated above.

However, this causation can itself be seen as part of a causal continuum that extends outward and backward from the individual and links, conceivably, with all causal chains spanning the entire history of the cosmos. This in fact is the position that a strictly deterministic philosophy must hold, and compatibilism is a form of determinism. If, then, causation of an all-embracing and global kind does obtain, the question will be asked: what real value or significance can be attached to the compatibilist notion of freedom? In other words, what point is there in saying that an individual is free when acting on his desires, if the latter are not of his own making and are merely links in a causal chain which totally transcends him and which is nothing less than cosmic?

This question clearly constitutes a powerful objection to the compatibilist definition of freedom. In meeting it, the following points need to be made: Firstly, freedom in the compatibilist sense, just as much as in the libertarian sense, fully accords with the political and civic concept of freedom. Politically and civically, the individual is said to be free when he is allowed to do what he wants to do, provided his actions do not encroach on the political freedom of other people to do the same, and provided they are not, in any additional way, harmful to others. Compatibilist freedom is, then, external and civic in character. As such, it has enormous relevance to political and social issues, especially in the predominantly modern context of democracy, with the latter's central concern for the liberty and integrity of the individual.

Secondly, a number of psychological and behavioural considerations need to be taken into account. Though a person's desires and aspirations are not of his own making or choosing, nevertheless they are what he prizes and loves. They are what no individual — at least, no self-respecting one — would ever wish to abandon. They constitute his identity, his essence.

Also, they actuate behaviour; it is in this sense that the person justifiably regards the actions he wishes to perform as being, just as much as their motives, *his own,* whatever their long-range antecedents. They are himself in action, his capacities in operation, his potentialities actualized. As exercises in the strength and power he possesses, they can be exhilarating and fulfilling to the highest degree.

Further, though both they and their motives are effects, they have identities separate from their causes. To be part of a causal continuum is not to be passive. For example, the heroic action caused by anger at injustice is precisely that: effects are *action*-outcomes of causes, with their own specific drive and momentum.[1]

Additionally, in any causal process, the factors involved are not conduits for some momentum driving the process independently of the factors in question. The latter *are* the momentum; they make it what it is; hence they do not transmit it. Thus determinism is always a matter of *parts* in action, with one part being affected by the previous one in a completely dependent and contingent manner.

This point must be borne in mind by those people who speak of 'pre-determination' in the form of the afore-mentioned momentum which is supposedly autonomous of particular and contingent factors. It is the latter, and they only, which constitute pre-determination, and all causality.

---

[1] The above argument for the active, rather than passive, character of a caused action finds reinforcement in Spinoza's concept of mental action as distinct from mental passion. In *The Ethics*, Spinoza defines a mental operation based on objective grasp of fact as an action, and an operation not based on objectivity as a passion (the latter word implying, by its first three letters, a kind of passivity). Now, if we argue that a physical action is caused by a mental action as defined by Spinoza, we can surely extend the idea of activity from cause to effect.

Further, the succession of particular factors is creative, a growth process. Causes fashion effects. Resultants flower from antecedents.[2] This clearly relates back to what has already been said about action-outcomes. Creativity co-exists with causality: the cerebro-neural causes of every brushstroke made by da Vinci in painting the 'Mona Lisa' do not in the least undermine the picture's status as a work of art and a creative achievement. Causes are fecund; and so are effects, with their capacity to become causes.

On the distinctness of identity possessed by effects: this distinctness is what the individual can cherish. Let the reader consult his own experience of fundamental self-encounter, self-discovery and self-description: the experience which leads him to say, of his most recurrent response-modes, "I find that I..." If he derives deep satisfaction from this experience, he should ask himself if that edification would be any the less profound if conclusive proof were provided that his selfhood was an effect, a product of causes. (This point relates to what was said earlier about the love the individual feels for his desires and aspirations.) For some people, yes, there would be a diminution in satisfaction: they would be distressed at the thought that they were not absolutely free. But for others, those for whom absolute freedom is not an issue, there would be no diminution. The difference, perhaps, is a matter of temperament; though questions of temperament are of course quite different from those of ontological precision—of ascertaining what precisely the facts are.

Returning to what has been said about the individual's cherishing of his desires and aspirations: that cherishing grounds his sense of ownership of, and attachment to, the qualities which comprise him; and, whatever the total causal picture, this sense is existentially vital. What the determinist does is to to *localise* the global perspective, to draw a line around a small area of it, and to declare that, to all intents and purposes, this area is indisputably himself.

In this perspective, very remote causal factors, such as those belonging to the early history of the cosmos, inevitably matter far less than proximate and immediate causes such as genetic inheritance and environmental / cultural influence. Though all causes are inter-linked, the proximate and immediate ones have by far the most significance operatively. The nearer they are to the action being produced, the closer they relate to, and the more they are actually part of, the agent's inner psychic metabolism: the more, in other words,

---

[2] Not least among these effects has been the emergence of human genius from the general process of biological evolution.

they are actually *him*. Conversely, the more distant the causes, the smaller the operational role they play. Hence it is false to argue, as some opponents of determinism do, that determinist reasoning leads to the ludicrous postulate that the entirety of cosmic causation is, *equally in all its parts*, the author of any one specific action.

It is local factors, then, and ones the agent is close enough to relate to, that produce internal motivation for action and the action itself. Prizing such motivation means, as a consequence, valuing the political freedom which allows the individual to express his internal promptings in outward action. The compatibilist will, if necessary, fight to obtain or maintain this liberty, as both a personal and collective right. Though compatibilist freedom is, as said, external and not internal in nature, the exterior political possession of it is crucial in the sphere of human relations and interaction.

Some Further Arguments for Determinism

The following arguments are supplementary to those made in the two previous essays, and to those in an essay entitled 'Some Arguments for Determinism', which appeared in my recent book, *Progressive Secular Society* (Exeter: Imprint Academic, 2008).[1]

In opposition to determinism, libertarians argue that moral thinking presumes uncaused actions, and that vital concepts in morality are void of content if determinism is correct in saying that all actions are caused. In this argument, the key word is "presumes". It suggests an fundamental weakness in the libertarian structure of thought: the weakness being that the structure is *a priori* and not *a posteriori*. By *a priori* is meant a focus on logical linkage between concepts, and a focus which precedes, or even excludes, actual empirical investigation. Conversely, by *a posteriori* is meant a focus on empirical investigation and its findings. Returning to the *a priori* rationale, this appears to be: 'Actions deserve praise or blame if they are uncaused. Hence praiseworthy and blameworthy actions are uncaused.' The latter statement is indicative, and a knowledge claim, in the sense that the word 'uncaused' is said to be the compliment of the subject of the verb. But the former statement is not a knowledge claim; its first verb ('deserve') conveys an opinion, while its second verb (though 'are') is part of a conditional, not an indicative, clause. Thus we have a knowledge-claim arising from what is *not* a knowledge-claim, or indeed from any statement about empirical investigation, but from an expression of moral attitude. This is a suspect procedure; and it lies at the heart of traditional libertarian reasoning, which has been repeated from generation to generation without, it seems, any recognition of the faultiness of the thought-structure.

---

[1] The reader is advised to consult this essay as essential background to the present material.

Libertarians may well take issue with the precise wording I have used in characterising their position; but if they accept that the characterisation itself is broadly accurate, and requires only some verbal modification, they still have to face the criticism that their thinking involves a false move to the making of knowledge-claims: that articulations of moral attitude, belief, or even dogma, invalidly precede, and attempt to ground, factual assertions.[2] By contrast, what determinism argues is that factual assertions[3] and empirical findings should be present in every step of the moral argument, and that the latter is in no way weakened by the former. Determinism takes this position because of its primary concern with scientific explanation of actions and events, which means identification of causes and effects. This concern is inextricably bound up with considerations of what action to take morally: action aimed at improving behaviour in the future.

The central role played by causal considerations in the effort to reform behaviour is definitively described by Russell:

> If we really believed that other people's actions did not have causes, we would never try to influence other people's actions: for such influence can only result if we know, more or less, what causes will produce the actions we desire. If we could never try to influence other people's actions ... argument, exhortation, and command would become mere idle breath. Thus almost all the actions with which morality is concerned would become irrational ... Most morality absolutely depends upon the assumption that volitions have causes, and nothing in morals is destroyed by this assumption.[a]

Also, mindfulness of causality precludes the error of thinking that, in any past situation, the course of events could have been different from what it actually was. To regard all past situations as inevitably taking the course they did is not, obviously, to condone or

---

[2] Here, I am mindful of Popper's powerful argument that every stage in the project of making factual claims is theory-laden. However, this argument applies solely to the business of making factual claims, so not to doing this in combination with expressing moral attitudes. In factual assertion, there is indeed the element which is, in the strict sense, non-factual: the theory-element, anterior to factual claim; and the presence of this element is acceptable, in fact unavoidable. But, again, this element is only to do with factual discourse, only epistemological. It is therefore not legitimately part of a moral perspective, and one being presented as a prelude to factual assertion. The attempt to articulate a moral outlook as a preliminary to making factual claims — as libertarians do — is completely invalid.

[3] Assertions always subject, of course, to the above Popperian considerations.

endorse them. They can still be morally censured; on the grounds, not that they could have been otherwise, but that *it would have been better* if they had been otherwise. In this way, a moral judgement is being applied to a causal sequence of events. Hence, in contrast to libertarian thinking, moral evaluation is being related to causality. The determinist has no problem in arguing that one causal sequence is morally better (or worse) than another; indeed, his efforts to reform behaviour are precisely efforts to instigate causal sequences in future conduct which will be morally better than causal sequences in past conduct. (In this regard, see again the Russell quotation.)

Further, the above wording "would have been better if they had been otherwise" calls for special attention. The deployment of this phrasing avoids the problem which would have arisen if the words "ought to have been otherwise" had been used. 'Ought' implies 'can', so "ought to have been" implies "could have been": implies, then, something which determinism rules out. Thus, the chosen wording conveys a wholly *moral* idea, whereas 'ought' phrasing would have conveyed a *factual* claim — again, that the past situation could have been different from what it was; and, as said, this claim is seen by determinists as invalid. The selected phrasing, then, avoids factual implications of any kind; it is nothing other than morally judgemental.[b]

Returning to factual considerations: determinism's causally-based viewpoint is diametrically opposed to the argument advanced by some libertarians that people makes deliberately capricious and random decisions; and that these decisions demonstrate absolute free-will. This argument brings to mind the alleged 'faits gratuits' celebrated by the novelist Andre Gide. Gide's 'deliberate capriciousness' was exercised in an attempt to prove his total freedom, but a valid way of interpreting this exercise is to say that it was *caused* by a desire to provide so-called 'proof' of such freedom. Also, is not the phrase 'deliberate capriciousness' a contradiction in terms, since caprice means no premeditation, no prior intention or forethought?

Libertarians frequently speak of the "everyday evidence of consciousness" to support their view that we possess absolute free-will. This argument has traditionally been one of the weakest aspects of the libertarian position, and it remains so. It raises the whole issue of possible discrepancy between an intuition or 'gut feeling' that we may have about the way things are, and the way things actually are. It is possible to continually receive a false impression. The development of modern science and philosophy has placed increasing emphasis on the *counter*-intuitive in its descriptions of how reality is structured. Moreover, modern psychology has foregrounded arguments about unconscious mental processes causing conscious ones. All these considerations cast doubt on the reliability of the "everyday evidence of consciousness".

Libertarianism is committed to denying moral value to any kind of causal continuity. No matter how intricately — or even agonisingly — complex that continuity may be, it is described by many libertarians pejoratively, in terms associated with automatonism and robotism. Accordingly, caused behaviour is never characterised as noble, beautiful or majestic. Hence, if it were proven conclusively that all the finest examples in history of bravery, generosity and altruism were resultants, the libertarian would be obliged to withold praise. To take one example: Martin Luther spoke words to the effect that he 'could do no other' than defy what he regarded as the corrupt power of the Papacy. He said he felt driven by an internal, self-impelled necessity to perform historic action. If he was correct in this self-analysis, then, as far as libertarians are concerned, he deserves no plaudits. For determinists, of course, the case is otherwise.

Again on the subject of causal continuity, the question should be asked: When the majority of people praise an action deemed heroic, how many of them consider whether the action was caused, and then, deciding it was, retract their praise? Many in fact do none of these things: which clearly indicates that their positive attitude has not been affected by considerations of causality. This is not to say that they should omit such considerations, since of course the latter are always taken account of by determinists; but it is to point out that people who do not take account of them are at least showing that their praise is not conditional on the view that the action was uncaused.

Further, when people do regard causality as operative, many then draw what is actually a deterministic conclusion: that the action resulted from the kind of person the agent is, and that the latter's character is as praiseworthy as the action it gave rise to.

The concept of character, or temperament/personality is deterministic because it denotes consistency of behaviour across a lifetime, and implies a cause (though not necessarily the only cause) for this consistency. How, on the other hand, is this consistency to be accounted for on the libertarian view that an absolutely free will is constantly being exercised? Libertarians might urge that each exercise of this will just happens, coincidentally, to precede the same or similar behaviour each time, and that the absence of totally chaotic, shapeless and unpredictable conduct is simply an empirical *given*, not subject to explanation. But clearly this is not the best of arguments. (Also, note that libertarianism is logically prevented from saying that the exercise of metaphysical free will *produces* the same or similar behaviour, since that would obviously be a causal claim.)

Ex hypothesi, libertarians are committed to denying 'character' as an explanation. Equally *ex hypothesi,* they are obliged to deny 'environmental / cultural influence' as an explanation. This is because they regard *all* attempts at explication as invalid. By contrast, 'character' and 'environment' are both seen by determinists as crucial considerations, and always inter-twined, in the attempt to account for behavioural consistency: an attempt, moreover, which they view as not only valid but absolutely requisite.

Libertarians frequently equate the notion of caused behaviour with that of behaviour which 'couldn't be helped'. Certainly it is the case that determinists do argue that conduct, in any given context, couldn't be helped, in the sense that it could not have been otherwise on that occasion. So, for determinists, such phrasing is meaningful and instructive. However, for libertarians, it is empty. As regards immoral behaviour, they see the wording as erroneous and unacceptable (though this still leaves the question of whether their view is scientifically-based). But as regards *moral* behaviour too, they are obliged to adopt the same position. (Again, this still leaves the question of scientific basis.)

This denial that moral behaviour is caused again shows the divergence between libertarianism and a large section of public opinion. How many members of the public, having witnessed an heroic action, will have a problem with the notion that the actor 'couldn't help' perform it? How many of them will, on the contrary, be gladdened and uplifted by the idea? How many will then say to the the actor: 'Please do go on not being able to help it.' A large number, I would suggest.

Such an attitude does not, of course, indicate that the public's view is any more scientific than that of libertarianism. But the attitude does at least show that the phrase 'couldn't help it' is capable of having positive connotations for some people, whereas for libertarians it has none. Further, if scientific analysis does indicate a complete causal continuity pervading the heroic action, then the phrasing will be fully vindicated in the scientific sense.

Finally, referring back to the determinist's aim of reforming the wrongdoer by attempting to instigate causal sequences which will produce better conduct, the objective is to elicit improved behaviour which the agent will indeed be unable to help performing. In this case, 'couldn't be helped' again carries positive connotations: though, once more, ones always subject to the results of scientific analysis of conduct.

End Note

[a] As quoted by A.J. Ayer in *Russell* (London: Fontana/ Collins, 1972), p. 119.

[b] The argument in this and the preceding paragraph is actually a correction of an erroneous line of reasoning which I advanced in a previous book, *Progessive Secular Society*. On p.46 of that text, in an essay on determinism, I contended that it was valid to maintain that a person ought to have acted otherwise on a previous occasion even though, on that occasion, he could not actually have done so. My reasoning was based on the view that a moral principle always ought to be upheld, and that the person had, on that occasion, failed to uphold it. Thus the 'ought' argument was a morally judgemental one only, and neglected to consider the factual aspects of the situation--namely the fact that the person could not have acted differently. In other words, I forgot the unbreakable linkage that exists between 'ought' and 'can,' therefore between 'ought to have' and 'could have.'

What is Ethical Rationality?
A Humanist Perspective

Reproduced, with amendments, by kind permission of the Editor of *The Ethical Record*.

A useful working definition of rationality is that it is a coherent system of thought, based on specific premises and leading to specific conclusions. The coherence from premise to conclusion must be unbroken. Each system has its own kind of validity; different premises lead to different kinds of coherence and internal consistency.

Let's see how this definition applies to *scientific* rationality. When people frame a scientific hypothesis, they do so in the hope of reaching a conclusion which, subject to empirical verification or falsification, will be the discovery of new facts[1] or a recognised non-discovery of them. They start from the premise of facts already known, or at least from the premise of what are generally regarded as known facts. Every step of the hypothesis must be consistent with that premise, and with the rules of logic; when this ceases to be the case, the hypothesis has demonstrably fallen into error and must be revised or abandoned.

Hence scientific rationality at the speculative, pre-empirical and pre-experimental stage, can find support only from existing knowledge. It is absolutely dependent on known facts and the relations between them. Later, at the empirical stage, the same reasoning will apply to the process of drawing conclusions from the data yielded by empirical investigation and experimentation.

This, then is one kind of rational consistency. Now let's turn to the kind that most concerns us here: *ethical* rationality. Like scientific thought, ethical reasoning begins with a premise and seeks to proceed coherently toward conclusions. But now arise the differences.

[1] In using the word 'fact', I am again mindful of Popper's argument that our conceptions of what is fact are theory-laden. This consideration will be implicit in all subsequent usage of factual terminology.

The conclusions are not discoveries of facts or confirmations of factual-claims, but recommendations on how we ought to behave; and the premises are not points of knowledge but values.

Values are not forms of scientific knowledge. They are convictions about what is regarded as good and desirable, or bad and undesirable, behaviour. Hence they are opinions, attitudes, feeling-positions. This is indeed all they can be, for, if a non-objectivist position[2] is held in ethics, we cannot know, in an objective and scientific sense, what is good and bad.

Values do not, like scientific facts, describe the world; they do not constitute information about the world's structure and processes. Of course, the fact that there are values is a point of information, and a study of their origin and influence provides information too; but the values themselves play no informative role.[3] Being non-scientific, assertions of value are not matters of proof or disproof and do not, like scientific statements, stand or fall on their correspondence with fact or (depending on which 'truth' theory is adhered to) on their internal coherence as factual discourse.

This means that no fact can be adduced to invalidate the view, for example, that it is good to treat other people as ends, not means. Such a view can legitimately be held even in the face of ample factual evidence that many people do actually treat others as means, not ends. The "It is good" part of the ethical assertion is independent of facts, because it evaluates, and so occupies a wholly separate space from that of science. By contrast, a morally evaluative component is no part of a scientific statement, and the latter enjoys no independence whatsoever from the constraints of fact.

Again, given a non-objectivist position in ethics, the implication is that the only location of values is the human mind. They exist nowhere else in the world, and so are not things the mind discovers as part of reality external to itself. This is clearly contrary to the arguments of moral objectivists, especially theists; objectivists do claim that values exist independently of the human mind and await discovery by the latter. By contrast, the non-objectivist view is that values are things human minds invent and then super-impose on external reality.

---

[2] This position, which I have argued for in my previous books, is widely held in contemporary philosophy.
[3] On this last point, I am in complete agreement with the views of (among others) Logical Positivists.

Moreover, values are what underpin moral argument and what give it *primary, foundational* validity. Although ethics does involve scientific reasoning, it does so only in a *secondary, relative* sense; it employs the discoveries and procedures of science only *instrumentally*, as a means to achieving ends and objectives which are themselves determined by values. Thus scientific reason can validate the method by which a moral purpose is fulfilled, but never the purpose itself, because the latter is, to repeat, value-based.

This links to a further fundamental difference between ethical and scientific discourse. The chief aim of ethical discourse is to advocate a course of action, and primarily by an appeal to feeling; whereas that of scientific discourse is to prove factual claims. Ethical argumentation may well engage in proving factual claims and in generally referring to facts, but it will do so only in the secondary, instrumental sense defined previously. In other words, it will do so only with reference to technical means for achieving moral ends.

In connection with the above : let's return to what was said about "It is good". An attempt is made by some thinkers to assign a primary and foundational role in ethics not only to scientific reason but to reason in a more general sense. Their argument runs as follows: It is good to act according to our nature. Morality is an expression of our nature as human beings. Therefore to act morally is to act rationally, because to act rationally is to act in accordance with our nature. So, to act immorally is to act irrationally, because it is to go against what we are.

However, this argument does not succeed in allocating a primary status to reason. Pervading the reasoning is the notion of *valuing* what we are; and it is surely this notion which leads to the emphasis on acting in accordance with what we are. Why, we might ask, should we act in accordance with what we are, instead of the converse? Why should we not go in for self-violation and self-distortion? If values arise from feeling, then valuing what we are is primarily a feeling-position, and not a position arrived at by a process of logical and ratiocinative thinking. Feeling is pre-rational. Valuing what we are is fundamentally a matter of respect, love and reverence for what we are; and these attitudes are not the product of rational thought. Rationality only comes in when we consider ways to protect and ensure the flourishing of what we love: comes in, then, only instrumentally.

As regards the origin of values: if neo-Darwinism is accepted, then values can be seen as arising from the feelings, sentiments, desires, drives, needs and aspirations which are the product of biological evolution; or, rather, which are the product of an inter-action between an evolved general potential for moral emotion and a particular environment which actualises that potential in a specific way.

Variety of environment must be stressed here, because it is this which accounts for the ethical diversity which is an undeniable fact both of the present-day world and of the past. If we assume that all human collectives are on the same level of biological evolution, we can also assume that they have the same emotional potential. Thus moral differences result from disparities in environmental circumstance, stimulus, pressure and conditioning: that is, in the ways emotion is elicited and channelled. Values have no other basis than emotion elicited and directed by environment. They are, to repeat, not objective because grounded in feeling, and because not forms of scientific knowledge.

The same point applies to human rights. The concept of human rights arises from a feeling-position and has no scientific status. Rights, of whatever kind, and including the right to exist, are mental creations and not discoveries made about anything in the world external to the mind. This observation does not of course invalidate the concept of rights as a *moral idea* and as a basis for political action, but it does refute it as a cognitive claim.

The distinction which has been insisted on so far, between what the mind creates and what it discovers, implies that there is a clear distinction between facts and values, and that this distinction is absolute. Values are feelings about facts: hence the two things are categorically separate. A value-term such as "good" or "bad" cannot be used in the same way as a fact-term; it therefore cannot be part of scientific description. There is a fundamental difference between giving a strictly factual account of an activity or situation which calls for moral appraisal, and actually making that appraisal.

However, in attempting strict description, we often find ourselves using value-terms, as if inescapably, but the importation of such terms is not legitimate. It blurs the distinction between facts and values and springs from the incorrect assumption that the moral epithets we apply to facts point to qualities inherent in those facts. (E.g. that a quality of "badness" is physically present in a particular action.) These considerations indicate that the task of formulating a descriptive mode of expression which is completely value-free is, in relation to our everyday use of language, a very difficult one.

Nietzsche, in *The Will to Power*, avers: "There are no moral phenomena; there is only a moral interpretation of phenomena." Thus, to describe the action of one man killing another man for money requires a vocabulary of information, one presenting knowledge of every event, physical and psychological, that occurs in the situation. But to pass judgement on the action requires a vocabulary of censure. Without exception, information can never function as moral appraisal, and appraisal never as information.

Also, no moral "ought" can be derived from a factual "is". All that can be justifiably derived from an "is" is another "is" i.e. a further fact in the sequence of description and explanation. Since science deals only with what is, the moral "ought" has no place in its activity. "Is" describes; "ought" prescribes. To move from description to prescription is to depart from the scientific sphere.

It is of course true that scientists do usually have an ethical commitment to seeking truth for its own sake, or to applying the knowledge they gain to the project of human betterment. In such cases, the moral "ought" is part of the general context in which they work. However, a distinction must be drawn between the motives for doing science and the actual business of doing it. That business is, again, to describe. Once more, the act of describing does not involve prescribing.

In contrast to the scientific sphere, then, the moral sphere is centrally and essentially prescriptive. Thus it is non-objective in the ways previously defined; so, subjective, or rather inter-subjective, because moral thought is collective and communal in nature:[4] Morality is a sharing of attitude on how people should behave.

Its communal quality is actually further confirmation of its basis in feeling. It seeks to be inclusive, and even universal; and this is because it is primarily concerned with the wellbeing of the group: not only with justice, order and security, as a purely legal system is, but with wellbeing in its fullest sense. This concern is a matter of feeling because the moral system wishes to bestow on everyone what it regards as the good. This applies in particular to what was previously said about human rights. The desire is to be maximally beneficial. It is feeling, not logic or detached ratiocination, which sustains the universality principle.

---

[4] So too, in fact, is scientific thought, but in a different way. Science is a sharing of knowledge, or at least a shared agreement on what constitutes knowledge.

The principle requires that the individual's actions should always relate, in some way, to the collective good. Also, it implies that the relation should be voluntary; although a moral system runs parallel, to a considerable degree, with a judicial one, it is non-judicial in that it asks for voluntary compliance (whereas a judicial system simply enforces compliance).

Given the inter-subjective character of values, in what way do they support the rationality to which they give rise? Here, the kind of coherence involved is, as previously said, that of means to ends: the rationale of technique. Once a value-premise has been established, it incurs a way of thinking which remains appropriate as long as it is technically compatible with the premise. For instance, the premise that it is good to survive and pass on one's genes produces a rationale of ways and means to ensure survival and procreation. Such coherence always aims at practical effectiveness, and so involves science, since objective knowledge of some sort, no matter how limited, is required for practical success.

However, the point made earlier needs to be emphasised: that the scientific content is incidental to the reasoning, and not its fundamentally validating factor. The latter is, to repeat, technical continuity with whatever the premise happens to be. Like scientific speculation, ethical reasoning must remain in agreement with something anterior to itself; but that something is not knowledge.

It may be objected that the criterion of simple technical continuity is inadequate when we come to consider dubious and sinister moralities. What sense is there, for example, in saying that the rationale employed by the Nazis to achieve their ends was appropriate because a logical consequence of their values? Alternatively, it might be argued that, if all ends and values are group-subjective, were not those of the Nazis just as legitimate as those of other (if larger and more normal) social groups?

In considering these questions, we must begin by conceding that, if there are no objectively right and wrong values, then all moral rationales are, in a strictly formal sense, on the same footing: each is relative and secondary, and each has a non-scientific source and starting-point in feeling. In this respect, then, the reasoning of the greatest moral sage is on a par with that built on the principle that it is good for a 'master race' to dominate the world, and by brute force and genocide. However, having acknowledged that there is no objective case for asserting the unacceptibility of Nazism, we can now to assert an inter-subjective one, based on feeling. To be emotionally repelled by the ends and means of Nazism is, we can argue, adequate grounds for opposing that doctrine and all others like it. If all values are inter-subjective, and if emotion underpins all moral systems, then feeling is all we effectively have as the foundation for attacking and defending those outlooks which we choose to attack and defend. Since the values of the Nazis were just as emotion-based as those of every other group, and since, on the strength of them, they embarked on a policy of aggression, they could have had no viable reply to the argument that, on the strength of different values, aggression was quite justifiably directed against them.

Let us note that the emotional repugnance underlying the inter-subjective case against Nazism is, like all emotion, an evolutionary product. Reference has previously been made to neo-Darwinism and the evolution of capacity for moral emotion. What can be added here is that the evolutionary process of natural selection has favoured the development and proliferation of capacity for those feelings which make for widespread mutual responsiveness and co-operation. They possess high survival-value. Hence these feelings have become the norm; and, in various forms and to various degrees, they are reflected in all widely-followed ethical codes, notwithstanding the various differences between these codes.

By contrast, the brutally exclusive emotions which motivated the Nazis were radically abnormal: aspects of states of mind which, in comparison with the norm, can be called unbalanced and pathological. This is why most people were and are opposed to them. It is psychologically inevitable that we will champion the norm we embody; not because what we are is 'right' but because it is fact.

Further, the values which conform to these norms cannot, on account of this conformity, be regarded as in any sense objective. They are certainly not so in terms of the definition given earlier. Another possible use of the word 'objective,' to mean in harmony with the facts of human psychology, is unacceptable because it fails to show why that harmony should not be a reason for calling the values subjective. Since the facts with which these values harmonise are essentially facts about emotional states, and since these states do not involve possession of normative knowledge, there is no reason to regard the values as objective.

"Objective" is sometimes used in an additional, related way, on the mistaken assumption that, because psychological norms are truths, the moral consequences of these norms must be a kind of moral "truth". Here, the word "truth" is being wrongly extended.

The moral effects of a psychological fact are actually part of that fact; they do not form a different category of truth. They remain features of a psychological situation, are completely circumscribed by it and can be explained in terms of it. In other words, the moral is inseparable from the psychological.

This point is not undermined by the fact that values are often embraced, not spontaneously, but as a result of argument; not accepted in a completely instinctive or untutored way, but inculcated by a process of reasoning. The point here is that this reasoning is not basically objective because its ultimate appeal is to the emotions. It is therefore, as said, a form of advocacy, therefore of persuasion; and it will be finally accepted or rejected on emotional grounds. Hence the response to the argument is a psychological event, one with moral components.

However, inter-subjective though morality is, it does admit use of the term "reasonable." It must immediately be added that this word has a scientific as well as an ethical application. To say, "This man is guilty beyond any reasonable doubt", is to use the word scientifically: that is, in connection with weighing up data and probabilities in order to arrive at an assertion of fact. But to say, "This is a reasonable way to behave," is to deploy the word ethically: not to assert a fact but to express a moral opinion. This statement, unlike the previous one, is not a deduction, not a factual conclusion drawn from available knowledge, but an expression of what is regarded as morally acceptable. Since ethical reason is primarily dependent not on facts but on values, "reasonable" behaviour is that deemed to be compatible with the values held by the person or group making the judgement. For instance, people who value social co-operation will appraise as "unreasonable" conduct which is socially disruptive; people who value physical health will think likewise about actions which threaten or damage health.

There can be a difference between viewing behaviour as unreasonable and viewing it as "illogical". The latter term is often used to imply that a person is not employing an effective technique to achieve ends which are themselves approved of. Given this specific usage, conduct will not be seen as both unreasonable and illogical. Unreasonable activity is based on ends which meet with disapproval; hence the means are one of two things being censured. With illogical action, on the other hand, the means are the only thing under censure.

From "unreasonable" and "illogical" to "irrational". The last term, I hasten to add, is not being used pejoratively, because here the meaning is "pre-rational" or "sub-rational". To repeat: values are not forms of knowledge or the outcome of a logical process of thought. Also, values, as modes of feeling, cause rationality without being the effect of it. Thus they are pre-rational or sub-rational, and in this sense can be called irrational. Values can be viewed, in fact, as being just as irrational as the biological circumstances which are the necessary condition for their formation.

As far as present knowledge shows, physical evolution has not been a rational process in the sense of being guided by an intelligent being, and one with a pre-established purpose to fulfil. Thus all its consequences share in a kind of original irrationality, and this includes human emotion and conduct. All derives ultimately from purposeless circumstance; all is founded on a causality which is mechanistic and not teleological. Hence the basic thrust and undercurrent of human existence is characterised by the absence of reason.

When we seek, through ethical practice, to lead balanced and effective lives, what we are actually doing is serving the irrational in the fullest way possible. The search for balance and happiness involves a process by which the intellect mediates between different feelings in order to secure the maximal possible satisfaction of them all. Intellect's ratification or censure of a particular volition is the upshot of a sub-rational situation in which various impulses have converged and produced either harmony or conflict. The situation requires a 'rational' response, either of acceptance or regulation, and the intellect acts accordingly. Rational activity is therefore a consequence; it is occasioned and required only by irrational interests, and its purpose is to minister to them and facilitate their collective operation. Reason, while playing a vital role in the overall psychic process, has a contingent status and so lacks a completely self-contained and self-referential sphere of operations. In other words, if there were no primal irrationality, there would be no subsequent rationality.

That primal irrationality pervades, as said, the entire evolutionary process. Through the latter, the dye of unreason has, so to speak, been cast. Thus future ethical thought, like present and past, will grow from the soil of the irrational and will remain, via environmental channelling, the voice of biological forces.

The primacy of unreason or pre-reason in human thought applies even to the practice of science. There are two reasons for doing science. One is for the practical and material benefits scientific knowledge brings. The other is for the sheer satisfaction of knowing. Both are grounded in feeling and value. The first involves valuing benefits because they ensure physical survival and enhance the pleasures and comforts of life. The second involves valuing knowledge for its own sake. Neither of these attitudes is derived from knowledge or reason. The former springs instinctively from the pre-rational will to live. The latter too is pre-rational since there is no purely rational basis for valuing knowledge *per se*; it is, in essence, an emotional commitment to truth, a love of truth, and, like all love, is not arrived at by a process of reasoning.

The attempt, incidentally, to establish a rational justification for truth-love by advancing the consequentialist argument that such love leads to honesty and truthfulness with oneself and others, succeeds only in establishing a non-rational justification; for when we consider why veracity is valued in the first place, we are led back to feeling and predilection.

The source of truth-love is probably neoteny, the evolutionary development by which man has inherited from his ape-like ancestors a brain structure similar to that of the ancestors at their infant stage. Such a structure results in greater natural inquisitiveness and curiosity than would have been the case had the brain structure of the ancestral adult been inherited instead. Now neoteny is a biological condition, mechanistically evolved by the natural selection process. As such, it automatically produces psychological consequences: states of mind which are not the upshot of ratiocination, even though they give rise to it. If, as seems likely, truth-love does emanate from such a state, it may justly be described as pre-rational.

To speak of the sub-rational mainsprings of scientific activity is not, of course, to deny the absolutely rational character of scientific reasoning as defined earlier. It is simply to note that, in science as much as in ethics, the irrational can produce the rational. It is, also, to distinguish between scientific rationality and the motives for pursuing that rationality. The former is, once again, dependent on knowledge, the latter not.

The role of the sub-rational in conduct has been one of the major themes in philosophy and psychology over the last 150 years. It has been stressed by, for example, Schopenhauer, Nietzsche, Bergson, Santayana, Freud and Pareto. Indeed, we can go back further than 150 years. In ethical philosophy, the primacy of the pre-rational was cogently summarised in 1751 by Hume when he observed, in *An*

Enquiry Concerning the Principles of Morals, that "morality is determined by sentiment". Hume of course did not have the benefit of a post-Darwinian perspective, whereas we, who do, can appreciate, in a biological sense, the full ramifications of his insight. The realisation that ethical rationality is necessarily relative must remain central to all circumspect humanists.

Assuming that human evolution will be an on-going process, what changes can be expected in the form that future moral reasoning will take? If it is true that biology is what primarily conditions psychology and morality, what mental alterations will accompany future physical change? We have in fact no way of knowing; but we can safely predict that evolution in the direction of greater physical complexity, which is chiefly neuro-cerebral complexity, will produce a wider emotional life and therefore a more intricate kind of moral sensibility. The function of ethical reason will then be to serve and harmonise an even greater number of sub-rational interests than exist now.

The result of this service will be a form of happiness appropriate only to the biological context in which it occurs. To quote Nietzsche again, this time from *Daybreak*: "every stage of evolution possesses a special and incomparable happiness neither higher nor lower but simply its own." Each phase of evolution is only capable of the kind of happiness which physical structure permits; and since evolution has no goal, no physical structure or concomitant kind of happiness can be considered superior or inferior to any other. None is nearer to or further from a state which could objectively be described as a summit of development. A process without an aim can have no culminating moment.

The corollary of this is that concepts of evolutionary progress and advance are not objective. 'Progress' is a value term, not a fact term. We may regard ourselves as more advanced than, say, *homo habilis,* because we enjoy the benefits and advantages (mainly in terms of mastery over the environment) which a more complex physical structure has given us. We like being what we are, and exercising the abilities we possess. It is because we enjoy these advantages that we value them—not the other way round—and this fact is another illustration of the way values are grounded in feeling. Future man will, no doubt, regard himself as more advanced than we are, but all he will be objectively entitled to say is that he is different—meaning, essentially, more complex. He will certainly value his greater complexity, but, to repeat, values are not forms of knowledge. This, moreover, is our own position in comparing ourselves with earlier forms of man. So, to be different is to be more, or less, complex; but it is only by inter-subjectively valuing complexity that human beings can go on to claim that to be more complex is to be "higher", and to be less complex "lower". As Russell wittily puts the matter, in *Mysticism and Logic:*

> Organic life, we are told, has developed gradually from the protozoon to the philosopher; and this development, we are assured, is indubitably an advance. Unfortunately, it is the philosopher, not the protozoon, who gives us this assurance.

In re-emphasising the dependence of values on feeling, I'd now like to take a closer look at a subject that was briefly mentioned earlier: the right to exist. That the concept of this right has no objective basis is clear from the fact that the entire phenomenon of life on earth is an accident, in the sense that it is the outcome of wholly mechanistic sequences of causation. Also, the concept is non-objective because based on feeling; and this is of course the case no matter how strong the feeling may be; sheer strength of emotion, here as always, is no argument for objectivity.

However, rationality can apply to the emotion underlying the concept. If we abandon the idea of a right to exist, and replace it with that of a *desire* to exist, we profitably exchage quasi-legalistic language for a language of pure feeling. Hence "we have a right to exist" becomes "we desire to exist, and therefore affirm the attitude that it is good to exist." This is followed by: "we will act on that affirmation in order to secure our existence." Here, then, is the typical ethical rationale: value-premise leading to a logic of technique. Emotion is acknowledged as lying at the root of life-affirmation, and everything else follows from that. The kind of language used to express this acknowledgement is, in a sense, primitive—the articulation of volition; but it arises from a sophisticated and penetrating insight not available to the person who employs quasi-legalistic terminology from simplistic belief in a right to life.

Let's now move on to a new area: the difference between moral assertions in general and statements which, while connected with morality, are of a fundamentally different type. A moral assertion, I would argue, is one championing a moral value; it advocates, on emotional grounds, that a particular ethos and the activity arising from it are good or bad, acceptable or unacceptable. The most obvious assertion of this sort is an unconditional statement such as "Benefitting people is good" or "Exploiting people is bad". At the same time, assertions containing a conditional element may also be moral if they imply commitments to values. For instance, "If you love someone, you ought to to be prepared to make sacrifices for that person." This statement implies that love is a good thing, and therefore that loving ought to involve ethical commitment.

On the other hand, there are some conditional statements which are not morally assertive because value-neutral in the ethical sense. For example, "If you love someone and if you think that love warrants personal sacrifices, then you ought to be prepared to make them." This is morally value-neutral because of the second 'if' clause. Its point is purely logical, and not ethical. It is saying that, if you feel a certain way and have a particular opinion about the way you feel, then you should, as a matter of logical consistency, accept the implications of that opinion. It refers to a moral value ("love warrants personal sacrifices") without either supporting or opposing it. Its "ought", then, is of the logical as distinct from the moral kind.

However, this is not to say that the statement is value-neutral in every sense. It does assert a value, and that is of adherence to logic. But of course logical values are not moral ones. Adherence to logic and nothing else can lead to ethically dubious contentions such as: "If you think that verbal offensiveness is sufficient justification for killing someone, you ought to shoot the man who has just called you a fool." This cannot be faulted for logical consistency, but it clashes with almost everybody's emotional attitudes. Another way the logical 'ought' can be employed is: "If you think it is good to be healthy and want to be healthy yourself, you ought to eat sufficiently nourishing food." Again, no moral value is being championed; no position is being taken on whether or not it is good to be healthy. All that is being stated is that, given a particular moral approach, other things follow from it logically and behaviourally.

I'd like now, in the light of the previous discussion on Nazism, to say something briefly about the emotional repugnance and moral outrage we feel toward certain actions and outlooks. The negative reaction stems partly from a sense of the challenge to our own complexity which the offending outlook or action constitutes. The latter's crudity or primitiveness is an affront to the depth, breadth and intricacy of feeling of which we know ourselves capable. Thus our repulsion is bound up with a sense of outspacing and transcending the mentality of the offender. It would not be felt so strongly if we did not value our own more complex and capacious state of being;

and the rationality we use to castigate the offender draws most of its strength from that value-feeling.

Finally, I'd like to draw some general conclusions from all the points made in this paper. Perhaps the most obvious one is that *science qua science can never offer moral guidance.* As has often been said, "Science can give you the facts but it can't tell you what to do with them." It is an illusion—and one that was particularly prominent in the nineteenth century—that science can become the ultimate arbiter in human affairs. It cannot, because always, prior to and along with knowledge, there are *attitudes* to knowledge. Only via these attitudes can facts have importance for us and influence us. Attitudes invariably stand between us and the data that science offers, and we can no more escape the former than we can our own shadows. Attitudes to knowledge are never formed by knowledge itself, precisely because they are anterior to it. Hence their origin and history are not dependent on the possession of scientific knowledge. Indeed, as we have seen, the pursuit of science is dependent on them. Thus *scientific rationality will always be located within the non-rational framework of values.* Further, this would remain the case even if (a very big "if") total and exhaustive knowledge were attained, since the central issue will invariably be, not facts, but our sense of the worth and significance of facts. That sense determines how we relate ourselves to knowledge, and knowledge to conduct.

The second conclusion is that, granted the primacy and inter-subjectivity of values, *humanism should always be aware of the problematic aspects of morality.* It must realise it will never know equivalents of the certainties and assurances which attach to objectivist ethics. In accepting the irrational basis of its morality, and in perceiving that there exist no value "truths" to be intuited or discovered, humanists experience anguish. Their moral choices and decisions cannot be vindicated by science, and there are no objective guidelines. Hence humanism is alone with its attitudes in a universe which is, as far as present knowledge shows, otherwise value-void. Its attitudes are ultimately all it has to work with, and it inevitably encounters extreme anxiety in coming to decisions which must be made on crucial matters of life and death. In abandoning all claim to objective knowledge of right and wrong, it sheds the protective coating of false certitude and so exposes itself to the iciness of a universe which is without mind: which not only offers no values itself but is unconscious of those which human beings create. With such a perspective, the humanist is no stranger not only to the perplexity previously defined but also to ways of resolving that perplexity, however difficult to reach those resolutions may be.

Lastly, *the aim of humanist ethics is to create a purposive order – a cosmos – from what is otherwise a chaos.* Because such an order serves human aims and needs, it can be described as an area of piloted non-rationality within an area of unpiloted non-rationality. As Santayana says in *Interpretations of Poetry and Religion*, "We are part of the blind energy behind Nature, but by virtue of that energy we impose our purposes on the part of Nature which we constitute or control." The imposition of purpose leads to ethical reason, which is, as it were, the compass the rest of the universe lacks. Every force in nature is engaged in a process of self-unfolding; but of these forces, only the human can bring rationality – deliberative, systematic and extended thought – to bear on the process.

The tasks and rewards of employing reason to minister to human aspirations are memorably described by Santayana, and it is with another quotation from him, again from the above-cited text, that I would like to close:

> We can turn from the stupefying contemplation of an alien universe to the building of our own house, knowing that, alien as it is, the universe has chanced to blow its energy also into our will and to allow itself to be partially dominated by our intelligence. Our mere existence, and the modicum of success we have attained in society, science and art are the living proofs of this human power. The exercise of this power is the task appointed for us by the indomitable promptings of our own spirit, a task in which we need not labour without hope.
>
> For as the various plants and animals have found foothold and room to grow, maintaining for long periods the life congenial to them, so the human race may be able to achieve something like its perfection and its ideal, maintaining for an indefinite time all that it values, not by virtue of an alleged intentional protection of Providence, but by its own watchful art and exceptional good fortune. The ideal is itself a function of the reality and cannot therefore be altogether out of harmony with the conditions of its own birth and persistence. Civilisation is precarious, but it need not be short-lived. Its inception is already a proof that there exists an equilibrium of forces which is favourable to its existence; and there is no reason to suppose this equilibrium to be less stable than that which keeps the planets revolving in their orbits. There is no impossibility therefore in the hope that the human will may have time to understand itself, and, having understood itself, to realise the objects of its rational desire ...
>
> What we should do is to make a modest inventory of our possessions and a just estimate of our powers in order to apply both,

with what strength we have, to the realisation of our ideals in society, in art, and in science. These will constitute our cosmos.[a]

A brief, final comment: when Santayana speaks of "rational desire", I take him to mean "realistic desire", that which is capable of realisation; *not* desire which originates in reason. The latter meaning would be at odds with his elsewhere-stated definition of man as the product of irrationality: with, that is, the true situation.

End Note

[a] For this and the previous Santayana quotation, see *Interpretations of Poetry and Religion* (New York: Harper Torchbook edition, 1957 (1900)), pp. 245-6.

Schopenhauer on the Basis of Morality

Reproduced by kind permission of the Editor of *The Ethical Record*.

There are a number of reasons for examining Schopenhauer's arguments about the basis of morality, and they have a good deal to do with the relevance of those arguments to present-day humanism. That relevance has been increasingly realized; the last 30 odd years have seen a marked revival of interest on the part of humanists (among others) in Schopenhauer's writings. The causes of this revival are too numerous to explore here, but a main factor has been a conspicuous decline in the rationalistic optimism—cultural, social and political—which was such a pronounced feature of many people's thinking in the two decades of intensively radical programmes of social reform that followed World War Two. A large amount of that initiative was led by humanists. Now, it is these people as much as anyone else who note as important and significant the complete absence of optimism in Schopenhauer, even though his position is widely regarded as actually too extreme. While rejecting extreme pessimism, most contemporary humanists also reject its opposite. The prevailing attitude now about general human possibilities is much more sober, cautious and qualified than it was in the period specified above, and in other periods as well.

Bound up with this reduction in optimism has been a recognition that extreme wilfulness in certain areas of human behaviour is a perennial problem, one that can never be completely resolved by social reform, no matter how ample the latter. This recognition lay at the heart of Schopenhauer's outlook, focussing as the latter did on the insight that willing and volition are the prime movers in human life, and intellect only secondary.

However, having said this, we must avoid drawing too sharp a distinction between will and intellect. Spinoza argues that will and intellect are simply different modes of thinking, because they both contain ideas: a volition is based on an idea just as much as a thought is. Hence volition and thought differ only in that the former leads to external (physical) action while the latter does not. Also, Nietzsche contends that willing consists of a complex of feeling and thinking, each being indispensable to volition. In the light of these views, we can define will or volition as a combination of thought and emotion from which external action emanates. Further, we can define non-volitional states as states of thought which may or may not involve emotion but which do not result in external action. To these states, the words 'contemplation' or 'meditation' are usually applied.

So, returning to Schopenhauer's viewpoint and the wording used to express it, what he regards as primary in human conduct can be characterized as, not the absence of thought, but a combination of thought and emotion producing external action. In turn, what he regards as secondary can be seen as, not necessarily the absence of feeling, but inner states which do not lead to external action.

Hence, what has previously been termed 'extreme wilfulness' can now be re-described as a volitional combination of thought and feeling which is altogether too narrow and exclusive—too selfish and self-interested—to constitute an adequate response to the complexity of the world. Such an attitude is, clearly, problematic. It remains a fundamental difficulty in many spheres of life, perhaps most prominently in economics and politics, where love of power and dominance, bound up with the relentless pursuit of material interests, continue to threaten democratic values and processes. In this connection, the international dimensions of organized crime might also be mentioned.

Schopenhauer's own sense of the problematic was so vast that it led to the extreme pessimism previously referred to. The latter is intimately connected with his insistence that the only genuine ethical emotion is compassion, fellow-feeling for other people's suffering, as the basis of the way we should act toward others. The focus on compassion stems from his view that suffering is actually the main component of human existence, its most recurrent feature, and therefore the central concern of morality. Further, it links with Schopenhauer's atheism, and in particular his rejection of the postulate pivotal to the three Semitic religions—Judaism, Christianity and Islam—that there exists a benign and all powerful deity.

On this crucial point about compassion, more will be said a little later. For the moment, I wish to link it with the general humanist perspective previously touched on. In arguing that an *emotion*—compassion—is the foundation of genuine morality, Schopenhauer echoes his eighteenth century predecessor, Hume, who avers that "morality is determined by sentiment."[a] Ethics, then, is based on something *human*: emotion, feeling, sensitivity. This is another way of saying that the source of ethics lies in mankind: a position which every humanist holds.

Clearly, to view morality in this way is to depart from theological ethics: that is, from the standpoint that ethics is and can only be validated with reference to the existence of deity—the latter being viewed as the fount and prime asserter of moral values. To reject this view is to reject the argument that theology is logically prior to ethics i.e. that comprehension of deity is a logical prerequisite for comprehension of good and evil. While such rejection can in fact be found in certain schools of religious thought, it is a universal feature of the thinking which dispenses altogether with theology. Thus, non-theological ethics is, by definition, non-cognitive with reference to deity: it does not make deity-referenced claims to know objectively what good and evil are. Such was Schopenhauer's position.

Additionally, Schopenhauer's emotivist position makes *no* objective claims whatsoever regarding knowledge of good and evil. This point is bound up with the fact that the emotivist outlook is sub-rational in origin. It has been previously argued that feeling and thought are intertwined in volition; and we can now consider this intertwining as the volitional consequence of a moral position which is at bottom emotional, *as distinct from* one which is fundamentally a matter of reasoning, of solely logical thinking committed to inductive or deductive method: as distinct, therefore, from the position postulated by foundational rationalists in ethical philosophy. Such a basis cannot be the source of moral values since, if Hume and Schopenhauer are correct, it cannot determine, be the cause of, a moral position.[1]

Thus the emotion-based position breaks not only with theological ethics but also with the rationalist tradition in morality which, in the West, goes back at least to Socrates. It must immediately be added that ethical rationalism is usually bound up with ethical cognitivism: which is, again, the doctrine that good and evil are things which can be objectively perceived, discovered.

Now, returning to Socrates: The Socratic tradition argues that wrong-doing is essentially the result of ignorance, lack of knowl-

---

[1] However, logical thinking can be deployed as a means to achieving the ends which a moral position involves. For this point, and for other related ones in this text, see previous essay, "What is Ethical Rationality?"

edge, the cognitive possession of which[2] would set the appropriate rational processes in motion, and so produce moral behaviour. This obviously contrasts with the view which is sub-rational, and non-cognitivist: the view that feeling, not systematic ratiocination or discovery of any kind, is the prime mover.

The sub-rational aspects of the above approach to ethics link it with much of modern psychology, which has extensively explored the non-rational factors in the human mind, in the process of abandoning wholly rationalistic models of the psyche. To this general movement of thought, Schopenhauer was a major contributor in the nineteenth century, and was praised for his insights by Freud and others in the twentieth century.

The sub-rationalist perspective finds reinforcement not only in modern psychology but also modern biology, with neo-Darwinism affirming that the human brain initially evolved as a survival mechanism, through a process driven by elementary will-drives inter-acting with environment: will-drives which in fact remain central to its operations. Here too, Schopenhauer is relevant: though writing before the publication of Darwin's *The Origin of Species*, and therefore unsupported by the extensive data of evolutionary biology, he himself saw the brain as originally a survival mechanism.

As has been previously implied, sub-rationalist ethics cannot, by definition, lay claim to scientific objectivity in the field of values: it cannot claim to have discovered what is right and wrong. Discovery is a rational and cognitive process, whereby factually accurate conclusions are reached on the basis of sense-experience, by either deductive or inductive method. But this process is no part of the sub-rationalist position, which focusses not on attempts at discovery of right and wrong, but on a psychological situation — a state of feeling — from which notions of right and wrong are viewed as emanating. The psychological situation itself is not judged to be rational, but neither is its non-rationality seen as in any way a weakness or defect. It is seen simply as an empirical *given*, from which all further thinking about ethics proceeds.

This means that the sub-rationalist perspective is in large measure a descriptive one. Further, though it is also prescriptive, it is not so in any *extrinsic* sense: it does not prescribe *from outside* the sphere it is describing. Its 'ought' is not, so to speak, a foreign importation, something being transferred from one sphere to another, in order to

---

[2] For Socrates himself, the cognitive centre of the moral outlook was the intellectual apprehension of the metaphysical Form or Idea of the Good.

change or transform the latter. Simply, what is prescribed is what is described. And what is described is how, in practice, people do behave ethically, as distinct from recommending how they ought to behave, irrespective of actual practice. Its prescriptions, then, always flow from behavioural fact, and recommend more of what already exists. Such a position is emphatically empirical, explanatory, grounded in experience, and therefore *a posteriori* in character as distinct from being *a priori*.

Such was Schopenhauer's position: one which, again, strikes a deep chord in modern humanism, bearing in mind that the latter is inescapably neo-Darwinian, and therefore bound to view moral phenomena to a large extent descriptively, in a causalist, evolutionary and historical framework.

The *a posteriori* temper of Schopenhauer's ethics is of course best expressed by the philosopher himself. In his seminal 1839 essay, *On the Basis of Morality*, the text from which the next and all subsequent quotations will come, he writes as follows:

> I shall probably be told that ethics is not concerned with how people actually behave, but that it is the science that states how they *ought* to behave. But this is the very principle which I deny, after showing clearly enough in the critical part of this essay that the concept of *ought*, the *imperative form* of ethics, applies solely to theological morality, and that outside this it loses all sense and meaning. I assume, on the other hand, that the purpose of ethics is to indicate, explain, and trace to its ultimate ground, the extremely varied behaviour of men from a moral point of view. Therefore there is no other way for discovering the foundation of ethics than the empirical, namely, to investigate whether there are generally any actions to which we must attribute *genuine moral worth*. Such will be the actions of voluntary justice, pure philanthropy, and real magnanimity. These are then to be regarded as a given phenomenon that we have to explain correctly, that is, trace to its true grounds. Consequently, we have to indicate the peculiar motive that moves men to actions of this kind ... This motive, together with the susceptibility to it, will be the ultimate ground of morality, and a knowledge of it will be the foundation of morals. This is the humble path to which I direct ethics; it contains no construction a priori, no absolute legislation for all rational beings *in abstracto* ... the foundation of morals that is reached on my path is upheld by experience, which daily and hourly affords its silent testimony in favour thereof.[b]

In his rejection of *a priori*, legislative and abstractly rationalistic styles of thinking about morality, Schopenhauer targets various aspects of Kantian ethics, as well as all theological approaches. The space left by what is discarded is adequately filled, in his view, by what he embraces as the true basis of ethics: as said, compassion, fellow-feeling and (an additional term) lovingkindness. This feeling is, he argues, truly disinterested and solely concerned with the weal and woe of the person whose predicament arouses it.

It is to be sharply distinguished, he insists, from other attitudes which may lead to what is apparently moral action. For example, a person may aid another in distress with the hope of incurring what he believes to be divine favour, and/or of being rewarded in an after-life, or perhaps of actually gaining an after-life as a result of his action. Further motives may include the desire for social approbation, social or political advancement, or in other ways for projecting an image which is advantageous to himself.

Moreover, obeying the law is not be assumed as evidence of a moral disposition. While one person may well follow the law and desist from injuring others because of a totally compassionate attitude, another person may be law-abiding merely from fear of detection and punishment if he were to commit a crime, plus the social stigma attached to these consequences. Hence what is in reality merely *strategic* or *prudential* behaviour must be differentiated from what is genuinely un-selfish and non-egoistic.

Overall, I think we should agree with this position, and regard authentic fellow-feeling as a true moral impetus. In doing so, we will accept Schopenhauer's distinction between the moral and the strategic.

Schopenhauer emphasises the point about un-selfishness because of what he sees as the enormous role played by egotism in human life. He describes egotism as "the chief and fundamental incentive in man", and as "boundless".[c] His view, an essentially Hobbesian one, is seen by many people, including myself, as exaggerated and therefore distorted, and as applying to only a minority of individuals, not the majority. The daily experience to which Schopenhauer himself so frequently appeals shows, in fact, that the majority are only moderate in personal aims, and more concerned with being part of a smooth-running collective whole than with pursuing individual ambitions to any extreme extent. They are not possessed by "boundless" ego-drives. Feeble, not pronounced, individuality is the rule: a fact which, indeed, Schopenhauer himself acknowledges, elsewhere in his work, in his famous phrase about the majority: 'Fabrikwaaren der Natur'.

At the same time, it has to be recognized that most people, while not exceedingly egoistic, are not exceedingly altruistic either. They are morally middling and average. Hence they do not serve as moral exemplars in the Schopenhauerian sense. Small-mindedness, rather than danger, is the main problem they present: a mentality which contains more in the way of strategic and prudential considerations, of a largely banal and innocuous kind, than radically disinterested ones.[3]

As regards the minority who are possessed of boundless egotism, to these Schopenhauer's words do indeed apply, and he performs a very valuable service in directing our attention to the dangers they present.

Given the above modifications to Schopenhauer's argument, I think we should agree with him completely when he says that it is only a few people who continuously evince compassionate and non-egoistic motivation in their dealings with others. While many people sometimes show a large measure of fellow-feeling, or frequently a small measure, it is only a minority for whom the feeling is regular and unstinting: for whom, then, it is veritably a way of life. These are, says Schopenhauer, "the people of true integrity, the few *aequi* (just)".[d] They consistently perform actions of moral worth which "leave behind a certain self-satisfaction, called the approbation of conscience". This feeling is to be contrasted with the "inner self-censure"[e] felt by people who perpetrate acts of injustice, uncharitableness, cruelty and malice, and who are capable of subsequently having misgivings about them.

In describing the compassionate mode of response, Schopenhauer writes very movingly, insisting that this mode is "original and immediate; it resides in human nature itself," and so "does not depend on pre-suppositions, concepts, religions, dogmas, myths, training and education".[f] Hence, he maintains, it cannot be taught, in the sense that the capacity for it cannot be implanted by education. This point is surely sound; education cannot create capacity, though of course it is a major agency for nurturing that capacity.

He avers that:

> In responding to another's suffering, we remain clearly conscious that *he* is the sufferer, not *we*, and it is precisely in *his* per-

---

[3] This perspective on the majority is succinctly conveyed by Socrates in Plato's dialogue *Crito*: "I only wish that ordinary people did have an unlimited capacity for doing harm; then they might have an unlimited capacity for doing good. Actually, they have neither."

son, not in ours, that we feel the suffering, to our grief and sorrow. We suffer *with* him and hence *in* him; we feel his pain as his ...[g]

Also: "I share the suffering in him, in spite of the fact that his skin does not enclose my nerves."[h]

Schopenhauer adds that it is only after the experience of compassion that genuinely-held moral principles of a general and abstract character can arise, as factors which will, in future, stabilize and control our behaviour, so that the latter follows a pattern which has already provided us with deeply emotional and instinctual satisfaction. In this argument, we again see his concurrence with Hume, regarding the foundational status of emotion in ethics. I myself share this concurrence.

As previously said, Schopenhauer's approach to ethics is primarily descriptive and explanatory. Thus far, he has described compassion — for him the fount of morality — as a component of human nature, a general human capacity (though not evenly spread). Further, the broad implication of his argument is that moral development consists in working with propensities which people already possess, cultivating what already exists internally, rather than attempting to impose moral directives from without. This implication, I would argue, is perfectly valid.

Now, more needs to be said about the descriptive and explanatory elements in Schopenhauer's thinking. What he goes on to do is to offer an explanation of *why* fellow-feeling is a human capacity: why, therefore, human beings are capable of lovingkindness.

His attempt at explanation takes us to the heart of his metaphysical doctrine, which is presented most fully in his main work, *The World as Will and Representation.* In its descriptions and explanations of human behaviour, this doctrine is pre-Darwinian (though in many ways strikingly anticipatory of Darwin). This point needs to be stressed because Schopenhauer makes no reference whatsoever to evolutionary genetics, a science initiated in the immediate post-Darwin period by Mendel. Hence he does not refer to those ways of thinking about mutuality in behaviour which have gained prominence since the 1970s through the work of Richard Dawkins. Dawkins argues that mutual sympathy and solicitude between people stem ultimately from the drive, shared unconsciously by every individual human being, to ensure the perpetuation, in certain other people, of his/ her genes. This means treating these other people with sensitivity. The various individual drives produce a collective momentum which results in a wider spread of sensitive behaviour than would otherwise be the case. Also, this effect is reinforced by the overall genetic similarities between individuals. (However, it should be added in passing, even if Dawkins's argument is broadly correct, it still has to be modified in the light of Schopenhauer's observations about the marked variegation in sympathetic behaviour among human beings.)

Returning to Schopenhauer's metaphysics: he thought that reality consisted of one thing only: what he called 'will'. It should be immediately pointed out that, in this context, the term is metaphysical one, not the psychological one that was used in the opening part of the essay. Hence it does not here mean psychological states or processes. 'Will' was for Schopenhauer *all* that existed in the objective, noumenal sense. The concept is actually akin to terminology in the world of physics, and Bryan Magee, in *The Philosophy of Schopenhauer* (1983) has cogently argued that the word 'energy', as used in modern physics, would be a suitable equivalent to 'will'. Much of the thinking in modern physics see energy as, in the words of Werner Heisenberg, "the primary substance of the world"; and this is how Schopenhauer saw 'will': an entity which was not only sub-psychological but also sub-biotic.

Schopenhauer went on to argue that 'will' manifested itself at the biological level as the will-to-live; and, in the case of human beings, at the psychological level as well, as 'willing' in the conventional psychological sense of that term. But his fundamental point remained that the will's essence lay deeper than any of its manifestations.

The 'will' was uncaused, and was not spatio-temporal. Space and time were themselves not objective realities but only constructions of the human mind. Also, the 'will' was undifferentiated. Though it appeared to have individual components, separated in space and time and causally inter-acting with each other, this was appearance only: not only because space and time were our mental constructs, but also because causality was as well. Hence, reality—the 'will'—was a complete unity, and only seemed to be a plurality.

Crucially, human beings were part of this unity. They only appeared to be separate from each other in space, time and causal context, but in actuality they were the same, undifferentiated substance:'will'. This essential unitariness explained the existence of compassion. People could genuinely feel for and with each other precisely because they were, at bottom, metaphysically one with each other. Moreover, recognition of this oneness between human beings — indeed, between all living things[4] — could inform the experience of compassion. Fellow-feeling could be a conduit for metaphysical insight. To feel for and with somebody was to feel for and with what could be perceived as yourself once more. You were the other person, and vice versa.

The linkage which Schopenhauer seeks to establish between ethics and metaphysics might initially suggest that his moral outlook is, after all, cognitive: not, of course, in a theological sense, but in the sense that it is founded on (alleged) *discovery* of how (godless) reality is structured, and therefore on discovery of how we ought to behave. If this were a true characterization of Schopenhauer's position, then he would of course be committing the naturalistic fallacy: he would be attempting to derive an 'ought' from an 'is', and hence be breaking the so-called 'law' attributed to Hume, a philosopher whom he greatly admired. But this is not what he is doing. Throughout his arguments, he gives central position to the emotional experience of compassion, as the starting point for everything else in the moral sphere. While he does indeed say that the experience can yield cognitive insight in the ontological sense, and provide a foundation for the methodical construction of moral principles, he all along insists on a point we have previously made: that the emotional experience must come *first*. The primary stage of moral commitment is, then, neither ontological insight nor ethical ideas. These arise as *consequences* of the experience; the ethical ideas as a direct result of the experience itself, the ontological insight as a result of the activity of the freely inquiring mind — an activity which stems from the experience.

Moreover, Schopenhauer points out that the experience of compassion does not always lead to metaphysical awareness, at least not in any extensive sense, and yet the experience does produce a consistent ethical commitment. He instances the example of an intellectually limited person who unfailingly acts in a compassionate and ethical manner but who never achieves, and never even thinks of achieving, advanced ontological insight. Thus for Schopenhauer, there is no necessary relation between moral capacity and intellectual. The former may exist without the latter, and — unfortunately —

---

[4] Schopenhauer, in contrast to Judaeo-Christian thought but in harmony with traditional Indian thought and, of course, with neo-Darwinism, averred the continuity between sub-human and human life.

vice versa. In these observations, Schopenhauer emphasises the primacy of emotion in ethics.

Further, returning to the issue of the naturalistic fallacy, Schopenhauer is arguing for an 'ought' from a *behavioural* 'is', and *not* from a general *ontological* 'is' i.e. not from a general postulate about the nature and structure of reality. The latter is usually the foundation for the argument that commits the naturalistic fallacy, but is not the basis of Schopenhauer's ethical position.

Now, in comment on Schopenhauer's metaphysical doctrine in relations to his ethics: It is of course an open question whether the doctrine is valid and, therefore, whether it offers an adequate explanation for compassion. If true, then it may well appear to furnish such an explanation; if untrue, then not. As for objections: an obvious one is that a person may feel compassion for another without being, or regarding himself as being, metaphysically identical with that other. Here, Hume's more limited argument about the exercise of sympathetic imagination by objectively-separate individuals is one that most people are more likely to agree with. Further, we should bear in mind the natural selection argument from evolutionary biology, according to which the evolved capacity for sympathetic response to others has been cumulatively selected for, since the lack of such capacity means more internecine conflict, so less chance of general survival. Capacity for mutuality has high survival value. Also, returning to Dawkins in this connection: we should note that his argument for the survival-drive of human genes has in its favour the facts that, firstly, it is much more modest in its ontological scope than is Schopenhauer's doctrine of undifferentiated and non-individualised 'will';[5] and secondly, it has a firm scientific grounding, in the data of evolutionary genetics.

Over and above objections to Schopenhauer's explanation for the existence of compassion, there are other strictures which need to be made. It can be argued that his focus on compassion as the sole component of morality is exclusionary. While virtually all of us, and especially humanists, would grant the enormous importance of this emotion, there is a case for saying that *other* attitudes and approaches, with their attendant activities, are also very important:

---

[5] It will be recalled that, earlier in the essay, a link was suggested between this 'will' and the 'energy' of modern physics, with 'energy' being seen by some physicists as ontologically primal. But — in objection to Schopenhauer's doctrine — a primal substance need not be undifferentiated: it may contain within itself a wide range of structural variations, variations so complex as to be, in certain senses, qualitatively different from each other.

attitudes which have an energising effect on the person to whom they are directed. Admiration; encouragement; praise; even sometimes a tough frankness meant to have a constructive and therapeutic effect: all these approaches—provided they are genuinely disinterested—have a place in a multi-directional moral context. That context is not, after all, solely concerned with palliating the effects of misfortune. It was noted earlier that Schopenhauer's exclusive emphasis on compassion was wedded to his extreme pessimism. This view, which sees little or nothing to be gained from endeavours to improve the world, is manifestly inadequate.

Related to this point is the observation that, for Schopenhauer, the disinterested exercise of compassion was bound up with an ultimate denial of the will. Compassion was aroused by suffering, and suffering was caused by willing. Hence, concomitant to the exercise of compassion was guidance toward a psychic state which no longer involved suffering and which therefore no longer called for compassion. (This state was closely akin to the 'nirvana' of Buddhism.)

Now denial of the will means, in the broad social and political context, the giving up of all effort at amelioration, since will is required for endeavour. Again, the unsatisfactoriness of this position is clear.

An additional point regarding effort at betterment is that the latter sometimes has to involve an actual *withholding* of compassion. In opposing people who are ruthlessly selfish, who display no compassion themselves, and who kill to get their way, there is no choice but to be equally ruthless, until such people have been subdued. Suffering and indeed death may have to be relentlessly inflicted on them until victory is achieved. Fellow-feeling can have no place in that project—which is, it should be remembered, a moral project in the fullest sense: to protect, preserve and enhance civilized values. Compassion is the foundation of the project, but it is compassion for those who are the victims of cruel and inhumane treatment. Lovingkindness in this direction dictates its absence in the opposite direction. As Sartre once said, to love a man is to hate the same enemy. So, if we accept this reasoning, we have to say that it is *qualified* compassion, not unqualified, which is in part the basis of morality.

Nonetheless, even while endorsing the above points, we can still regard Schopenhauer's central concern with fellow-feeling for suffering as a strength as well as a limitation. Its strength resides in the fact that compassion is always in short supply in the world; more is always needed than actually exists. Though most of us do not subscribe to Schopenhauer's total pessimism, we must at the same time acknowledge the formidable extent of the suffering that does obtain: pain of all kinds, in all societies, remediable and irremediable. In particular, we should recognize the tribulation caused by extreme poverty, deprivation of opportunity, political oppression, racial and ethnic persecution, and war: much of this being the result of extreme wilfulness and the absence of compassion, and none of it, world-wide, decreasing to any major extent. It perhaps goes without saying that cognition of these ills reduces self-preoccupation in the process of widening responsiveness to others. Responsiveness should of course lead to action to improve the situation; and — returning a last time to the subject of humanism — for humanists, mankind is the only agency which can effect such amelioration. The fundamental need for sympathy is nowhere more powerfully conveyed than in Schopenhauer's writings; and from these the humanist activist may draw inspiration almost to the same extent as he does from the work of philosophers with strongly constructive outlooks.

End Notes

[a] *Enquiry Concerning the Principles of Morals*, Appendix 1.
[b] *On the Basis of Morality*, trans. E.F.J. Payne (Indianapolis/Cambridge: Hackett Publishing Company, 1995 (1839)), p. 130.
[c] *Ibid.*, p. 131
[d] *Ibid.*, p. 139
[e] *Ibid.*, p. 140
[f] *Ibid.*, pp. 148–9
[g] *Ibid.*, p. 147
[h] *Ibid.*, p. 166

Bertrand Russell and James Thomson

I will briefly compare Russell's renowned essay 'A Free Man's Worship' (1903) with a key extract from Thomson's most important poem *The City of Dreadful Night* (1874). The comparison shows basic similarities between the two works, even though they are thirty years apart. In fact, despite the time-distance, they clearly belong to the same intellectual climate: that of the late nineteenth and early twentieth centuries, when many of the most advanced minds in Britain and the rest of the Western world were atheistic or at least agnostic, feeling as they did the full impact of the findings of science.

Both the Russell and the Thomson show that the registering of this impact was an austerely demanding, indeed transforming experience. The sense of the cosmos as a godless phenomenon — mindless, non-moral, without purpose — penetrated to the core of their being. This is evident partly from the way they came to view the universe as essentially a place of darkness, despite the many suns it contains. Thomson sees humanity as "battling in black floods without an ark" and as "spectral wanderers of unholy Night ... withdrawn from joy and light!".[a] Similarly, Russell sees mankind as situated on "a narrow raft illumined by the flickering light of human comradeship"; surrounding this raft is "the dark ocean on whose rolling waves we toss for a brief hour".[b] Also, Russell defines human beings as "fellow sufferers in the same darkness".

Thomson declares that the cosmos is non-moral: "I find no hint throughout the Universe/Of good or ill, of blessing or of curse." This is echoed by Russell when he describes the cosmic process as "Blind to good and evil," (unlike man, who, according to Russell, possesses knowledge of good and evil[1]).

Further, both writers stress the brevity of human life, as perceived within the framework (or, as Russell says, "scaffolding") of the grim truths which science has disclosed. Thomson avers: "all our wretched race/Shall finish with its cycle, and give place/To other beings, with their own time-doom". Likewise, Russell speaks of

---

[1] At this stage of his career, Russell was a moral cognitivist.

man's "brief years" and "little day" (a period in which, however, he is free to discover as much as possible about the cosmos.)

There are of course differences between the two pieces. Russell explores in detail the moral implications of the cosmic perspective he presents, while Thomson does not (at least, in the extract under consideration). As part of this exploration, Russell speaks poignantly of the importance of art and philosophy; again, this is not in Thomson. Yet despite these disparities, the pieces can — as said — be paired as leading expressions of the unflinching atheism which was so prominent a feature of the period in which the two men were writing.

Other leading expressions are to be found in the writings of Santayana and Thomas Hardy, and these can be set directly alongside the words of Russell and Thomson. For example, Russell contends that man is "the product of causes which had no prevision of the end they were achieving," and that "his origin, his growth, his hopes and fears, his loves and his beliefs, are but the outcome of accidental collocations of atoms". He adds that "all the labours of the ages … all the noonday brightness of human genius, are destined to extinction in the vast death of the solar system". This should be compared with Santayana's definition of man as "the product and the captive of an irrational engine called the universe".[c] Likewise, Thomson and Hardy can be juxtaposed. Thomson describes an atheistic preacher with "Two steadfast and incomparable eyes/Burning beneath a broad and rugged brow". This bears a striking resemblance to a phrase of Hardy's, in his 1910 poem, 'A Plaint to Man': "the deicide eyes of seers".

These writers and others, working in the half century after the publication of Darwin's *Origin of Species*, and witnessing the steady accumulation of general scientific evidence that confirmed the Russell / Santayana definition of man, represent a position from which there can be no legitimate retreat. This point must be insisted on, given the recent resurgence in religious fundamentalism, and the increasing tendency among some influential groups in Western society to display an over-accommodating and insufficiently critical attitude toward religious beliefs. The scientific solidity and authority epitomised in Russell's writings in particular are qualities which must be retained.

Also, their retention gives their possessors a right undeserved by those who lack them. It is a right which Russell delineates in his essay: the right to panoramic joy and happiness, when the latter have a valid ontological foundation. Russell argues that a cosmic perspective which is truly scientific must lead to a renunciation of desire for personal goods, since these are "subject to the mutations of Time". Renunciation is also called for by the recognition that "the world was not made for us". However, renunciation is not an end in itself but a path "to the daylight of wisdom, by whose radiance a new insight, a new joy, a new tenderness, shine forth to gladden the pilgrim's heart". This inspiring and sustaining outlook is actually a state of mental mastery "over the thoughtless forces of Nature"; by understanding these forces fully, by perceiving even their physical omnipotence, one achieves mental superiority over them. They are cognitively absorbed, assimilated, and so lose their power to terrify or dismay. Likewise with the sorrow and pain with which human existence is fraught: "to feel these things and to know them is to conquer them".

This internal victory over the adversity of external fact constitutes a kind of cognitive heroism, and is "the true baptism into the glorious company of heroes, the true initiation into the over-mastering beauty of human existence". (Manifestly, Russell does see positive elements in human experience as well as negative ones, as shown here and in his references to genius and cultural heritage.) From the triumph, "renunciation, wisdom and charity are born; and with their birth, a new life begins". The new life means "to burn with passion for eternal things," and so gain a freedom which attachment to the merely personal and temporary can never give. Such burning is "the free man's worship". (In these words, we are inevitably reminded of Spinoza's *sub specie aeternatis*. Spinoza was in fact a major influence on Russell.)

The hard-won, purified, scientifically endorsed joy which Russell describes is the rightful reward of everyone who has consistently trod the scientific path, and steadily shed illusions. That path constantly demands toil, is constantly upward, and is unsparing in many of the vistas it unfolds. At the same time, being equal to its exigencies is a source of profound satisfaction; possessing the unflagging zeal to move higher and higher is the foundation of happiness. Salvation lies in finding joy in the truth, says Santayana. If we free the word 'salvation' from its supernaturalistic associations, and use it in the way Santayana does, to mean optimal being; if we are also mindful of another of Santayana's statements, that intelligence is the highest form of vitality; then for the secularist this concept of salvation is surely non-controversial. Thus the daylight of wisdom to which Russell refers can be fully and legitimately enjoyed. This is so despite the knowledge that such enjoyment is bounded by darkness — of those areas of the universe forever untouched by sunlight, and of personal death.

End Notes

[a] These and all other quotations from the poem are taken from *The Oxford Anthology of English Literature*, Volume II, general eds. Frank Kermode and John Hollander (Oxford University Press, 1973), pp. 1491-3.

[b] These and all other quotations from the essay are taken from *The Basic Writings of Bertrand Russell*, ed. Robert E. Egner and Lester E. Denonn (London: George Allen and Unwin Ltd., 1962 (1961)), pp. 66-72.

[c] From *Interpretations of Poetry and Religion*, p. 241.

Russell and Santayana

The previous essay, chiefly comparing Bertrand Russell with James Thomson, also contained a comparison between Russell and Santayana, in connection with ideas expressed by Russell in his essay 'A Free Man's Worship'. I now wish to enlarge on this comparison.

In an earlier book, *Spinozan Power*,[a] I drew attention to the fact that, at the turn of the twentieth century, Russell and Santayana, two of the leading modern philosophers,[1] presented a definitive picture of man's position in the universe: Russell in, again, 'A Free Man's Worship', and Santayana in the essay 'A Religion of Disillusion' (1900).[b] Both described man as product of mindless cosmic processes whose further unfolding would incur his destruction. This view, which was still relatively new and challenging in the early 1900s, is now the orthodoxy of secular science, and a key element in atheistic existentialism. In addition, it now occupies a sizeable space in the general consciousness.

The value of the two essays lies not only in their confronting, with unflagging courage, the grim cosmic reality. It resides also in their positive statements on the inspiration and sustenance still available to man after he has fully absorbed the vast cosmic facts, and shed the illusions of deity, soul and immortality of soul. In Russell, the call is to assert human solidarity, and maintain compassionate and civilised values in the face of a brute universe devoid of them. In Santayana, the argument is vsirtually the same, but more extensive, urging the creation of a specifically human order—social, artistic, scientific—as a riposte to the outer cosmic chaos. In these views, the contemporary position is again prefigured: the perspective of all present-day humanists is that humanity can only establish its context in contradistinction to the surrounding cosmos.

The definitiveness of these statements of a century ago does not however mean that they are without precedent. In fact, their strength derives from a tradition in Western philosophy going back to the early nineteenth century. The work of the major atheistic thinkers of that century, including Schopenhauer, Feuerbach, Marx, Nietzsche, Comte and Spencer, is broadly, compositely, echoed in Russell and Santayana as the latter take up the nineteenth century heritage, filter it through the medium of their own sensibilities, and then turn their

---

[1] Russell's dates are 1872–1970, and Santayana's 1863–1952.

faces to the new century. Spencer in particular was a strong influence on both, and Schopenhauer an additional one on Santayana.

It should be added that the nineteenth century inheritance was not the only one on which the two philosophers drew. They also looked to the pre-Socratic Greek, and to Democritus in particular. Both praised the open-minded and rationalistic vigour of pre-Socratic thought, establishing as it did the foundations of the scientific outlook in the West. As regards Democritus: he was one of the two philosophers whom Santayana valued most highly, the other being Aristotle. Santayana shared with Democritus a materialistic and mechanistic viewpoint.[c] Russell also lauded Democritus, regarding him as the last of the ancient Greek philosophers to engage in a genuinely disinterested and scientific effort to understand the world.[d]

A further point in common between the two men was their dislike of an extremely functionalist attitude toward the individual. Both were liberal individualists, hostile to social pressures which deny the complexity of the personal sphere and threaten its integrity. Hence they were opposed to viewing the individual largely in terms of his social and occupational role. They both criticised their contemporary, John Dewey, for allegedly having a functionalist perspective. Russell quoted with approval Santayana's charge that "In Dewey ... there is a pervasive quasi-Hegelian tendency to dissolve the individual into his social functions".[e]

In connection with the integrity of the individual sphere, both valued outstanding individuality and genius. They were unembarrassed advocates of the uncommon. Santayana writes:

> Beauty, genius, holiness ... radiate their virtue and make the world in which they exist a better and more joyful place to live in. Hence ... the universal interest in whatever is extraordinary ... shows the need men have of distinction and the advantage they find even in conceiving it.[f]

And Russell avers:

> We are so persuaded that we live in the Age of the Common Man that men become common even when they might be otherwise ... All forms of greatness ... share a certain quality, and I do not wish to see this quality ironed out by the worship of mediocrity.[g]

Santayana's previous reference to Hegel leads to another area of agreement between the two philosophers. Both rejected Hegel's view of history as a linear progression moving toward a final, consummate term: the view of history, then, as possessing laws—in this case, laws of linear progression. Santayana bluntly avers that so-called historical laws reduce in fact to physical laws, and that "Every 'historical force' pompously appealed to breaks up on inspection into a cataract of miscellaneous natural processes and minute particular causes. It breaks up into its mechanical constituents ..."[h] Likewise, Russell contends that historical processes are always multi-factorial, that they lead to no final state in human affairs, and that "the fundamental study in searching for historical causes is hydrography."[i]

Moreover, both philosophers had a very strong orientation toward science (which included critiquing scientific method). Hence they both rejected as unscientific Henri Bergson's doctrines of a 'life-force' (*élan vital*) which allegedly exists independently of matter, and of 'creative evolution'—that is, evolution developing in ways other than those of genetic mutation and natural selection (the latter being the generally accepted tenets of neo-Darwinism).

Finally, regarding what was said earlier about their views of man in relation to the cosmos as a whole, both laid great stress on not making knowledge-claims, especially cosmological ones, without sufficient justification. They emphasised the limitations of present human knowledge, and urged the need to proceed with extreme care and diligence—always along the path of science—in the effort to gain further knowledge. This is clear from Russell's words, "all human knowledge is uncertain, inexact and partial."[j] It is equally evident in the words of Santayana: "the truth is remote, difficult, and almost undiscoverable by human efforts ..."[k]

End Notes

[a] *Spinozan Power in a Naturalistic Perspective*, T. Rubens (London: Janus Publishing Co., 1996), pp. 12–13.

[b] Source details for 'A Free Man's Worship' were given in the previous essay. The Santayana can be found in *Interpretations of Poetry and Religion*.

[c] For his references to Democritus, see especially *Reason in Science* (New York: Dover Publications Inc. edition, 1983 (1906)), pp. 69–84.

[d] See *History of Western Philosophy* (London: Unwin University Books edition, 1975 (1946)), p. 89.

[e] *Ibid.*, p. 781.

[f] *Reason in Society*, p. 90

[g] *Basic Writings*, pp. 539–40.

[h] *Reason in Science*, p. 54, 57

[i] *Basic Writings*, p. 510, 536

[j] As quoted by John Passmore in *A Hundred Years of Philosophy* (Penguin Books, 1966 (1957)), p. 239.

[k] In *The Wisdom of Santayana* (London: Peter Owen Ltd., 1964), p. 111.

Santayana and Hardy

Born just under a generation apart—Hardy in 1840 and Santayana in 1863—both came to intellectual maturity in the period when Darwinism in particular and nineteenth century science in general were at the height of their impact; and, on both men, the impact was decisive.

Also, the impact was on two outlooks that were strikingly similar. Both men, while fully accepting that science had destroyed the ontological claims made by Christianity, retained a deep-seated orientation toward religious culture. This was bound up with their poetic propensities. Hardy of course was and remains a major poet. Santayana too wrote poetry (though without achieving eminence) and, more distinctively, wrote about poets (mainly Lucretius, Dante, and Goethe). With both, a keen poetic sense helped them to the insight that religious doctrines, especially Christianity, could still be valued despite the refutation of their ontologies: could be valued as allegorical and symbolic expressions of moral perspectives—as, therefore, moral statements in poetic form.

This view of the allegorical importance of religion has since come to be quite widely held by secularists, but it is worth remarking that Hardy and Santayana were among its earlier adherents: an indication of the influence on them of the massive reconstruction in ways of thinking about religion which distinguishes the nineteenth century. They were affected by many thinkers, but perhaps most of all by Schopenhauer, whose arguments for religion's allegorical status had been fully formulated by mid-century and were to increase in currency by the end of the century.

Santayana's sense of the linkage between poetry and religion is clear simply from the wording of the title of one of his books, *Interpretations of Poetry and Religion*. It is also evident at many points in his work overall. As a main generalisation, he avers that "Religion is human experience interpreted by human imagination". He goes on to say:

> The idea that religion contains a literal, not a symbolic representation of truth and life is simply an impossible idea. Whoever entertains it has not come within the region of profitable philosophising on that subject.

Hence the appropriate approach to religious narratives is to "honour the piety and understand the poetry embodies in these fables".[a]

As a philosopher, Santayana wrote extensively and systematically on religion's moral and poetic status. The same is not true of Hardy, who was not a philosopher in the strict sense of the term, and whose views on religion were expressed in sporadic and fragmentary manner. Nevertheless, there are moments when Hardy delineates his position with powerful conciseness, as in the following: "poetry and religion [the latter in its "essential and undogmatic sense"] touch each other, or rather modulate into each other; are, indeed, often but different names for the same thing ..." Here, Hardy seems to define religion as basically a source of moral inspiration. This interpretation sits well with what he goes on to say about "an alliance between religion, which must be retained unless the world is to perish, and complete rationality, which must come, unless also the world is to perish, by means of the interfusing effect of poetry ..."[b] If religion and rationality are compatible, as Hardy says they are, then this can surely only be the case if religion is essentially moral and not magical or miraculous in content.

In addition, though, we should note Hardy's double concept of religion, not found in Santayana. He initially defines it as often the same thing as poetry; but then as something separate from poetry — by which, however, it may be infused, in the attempt to ally it with rationality.[1]

This is a variation on Santayana, but not one significantly lessening the affinity between the two men. That affinity went, indeed, beyond their large measure of agreement on the subject we have been examining. I would, in conclusion, like to say something about their temperaments and the respective tones of their writing.

---

[1] The general notion of linkage between poetry and religion which Hardy and Santayana explored was also momentously examined, in the later nineteenth century, by Arnold and Ibsen.

Arnold wrote: "The strongest part of our religion today is its unconscious poetry ... A religion without poetry ... is no religion at all ... most of what now passes with us for religion and philosophy will be replaced by poetry ..." (As quoted by Basil Willey, *Nineteenth Century Studies* (Penguin Books edition, 1964 (1949)), pp. 288-9.)

Ibsen averred: "I believe that poetry, philosophy and religion will be merged into a new category and become a new vital force, of which we who are now living can have no clear conception." (In *Ibsen: Letters and Speeches*, ed. Evert Sprinchorn (New York: Macgibbon and Kee, 1965), p. 267.)

Both men clearly had a melancholy tendency. With Hardy, one of the most frequent comments made by literary critics about his world-view is that it is pessimistic. Hardy himself actually denied this, arguing that what others called pessimism he regarded as "'questionings' in the exploration of reality", ones justified on the grounds that "If a way to the Better there be, it exacts a full look at the Worst".[c] However, even if Hardy's argument is accepted, there can be little doubt that his interest in "the Worst" was a major feature of his work.

Regarding Santayana too, let's look at his own words: "That life is worth living is the most necessary of assumptions, and, were it not assumed, the most impossible of conclusions." Also, "There is tragedy in perfection, because the universe in which perfection arises is itself imperfect."[d] It is of course the case that, as with Hardy, the note of sadness does not continually sound; but it is never far away, and we are never surprised when we do hear it.

In reading the prose of both writers (and I'm now focussing on prose because this, as well as being Santayana's main medium, was also the one in which Hardy — with the exception of his epic poem *The Dynasts* — gave the most extensive expression to his philosophical views) we are continually mindful of a complete absence of shrillness and stridency in tone. Their work is always measured, controlled, and without any attempt at emotional forcing. It frequently possesses a classic and statuesque quality.

In this way, both writers may be deemed exemplary. In accepting the allegorical character of religion, they found no alternative source of cosmic assurance to that which religious literalism had once purported to provide. They nonetheless maintained composure: a composure hard-won, stoical and dignified. It is arguable, from long experience, that the need for such steadfastness is paramount in all those who share the atheistic outlook and use the written word to convey it. Santayana and Hardy can be numbered among those who are pivotal in meeting that need.

End Notes

[a]   For all quotations, see Will Durant, *The Story of Philosophy* (London: Ernest Benn Ltd., 1955 (1947)), p. 427.
[b]   For both quotations, see *Thomas Hardy: Selected Shorter Poems*, selected by John Wain (London: Macmillan 'Papermac', 1966), pp. 124–5.
[c]   *Ibid.*, p. 120.
[d]   For both quotations, see Durant, *op. cit.*, p. 432.

Santayana and Schopenhauer

Since so many references have already been made to these two philosophers, it is now appropriate to compare them in some detail. Mention has previously been made, in the essay 'Santayana and Hardy', of the fact that Santayana concurred with Schopenhauer's view that the ontological doctrines of the various religions possessed not literal but poetical value. In fact, this concurrence is the most prominent similarity between the two thinkers, writing though they were almost a century apart: Schopenhauer in the early to mid nineteenth century, and Santayana in the early to mid twentieth. Both were enormously knowledgeable about the world religions; and, though both atheists, combined their erudition and critical approach with a deeply empathetic engagement with their subject. In essence, both saw religious culture as a highly significant aspect of human history and development.

A case could be made for saying that, of leading Western philosophers of the last 200 years, they are the two most informative on religion as a cultural phenomenon. Santayana, among many references, devoted three full-length books to the subject: the afore-mentioned *Interpretations of Poetry and Religion,* plus *Reason in Religion* and *The Idea of Christ in the Gospels*. Schopenhauer, for his part, was never far from treatments of religion in his immense volumes, especially in his essays.

The linkage the two men establish between religious ontology and poetry means that they view religion as offering a picture of the origin and structure of the universe—one which is highly imaginative and poetic in character, and which is thought by its adherents to be literally, scientifically true, when in fact it is not. It is false science. However, despite this, it remains impressive and moving as an imaginative achievement.[1]

Similarly moving, they say, is religion's ethical dimension, linked as it is to the ontological. But the same point applies. Because most religions connect ethical values with various ontological

---

[1] Broadly in this connection, see additional points about religion and poetry in the 'Santayana and Hardy' essay.

claims — chiefly, the one that there exists a deity which has created or at least endorsed moral values — the problem of false, or at any rate dubious, scientific assertions attaches as much to the ethical aspect of religion as to the ontological.

Both Santayana and Schopenhauer aver that, for all advanced minds in the Western context, religious ontology has had its day.[a] Further, they argue that what is of value in religious ethics must now be incorporated into a non-religious perspective. In this, they are both in accordance with most advanced minds in modern Western culture: that is, with minds which evince unflagging scupulousness in the scientific, logical and critical senses. Moreover, we should in passing note the historic position occupied by Schopenhauer's thinking, as precursor to Santayana's. His prediction about the demise of religious thought in the West has been borne out in the work, not only of Santayana but also of most of the major Western thinkers since his day: for example, Marx, Spencer, Nietzsche, Russell, Dewey and Sartre.

His specific influence on Santayana is evident not only in the above regard but also in the very terminology which Santayana deploys, in the course of conveying the completely naturalistic outlook which is, for him,[2] the consequence of rejecting religious ontology. Schopenhauer uses the term 'will', in the psychological sense,[3] to mean volitional capacity and propensity; and Santayana broadly adopts this usage. Thus, to quote words previously cited in the essay 'What is Ethical Rationality?', Santayana speaks of the universe's having blown its energy "into our will," and expresses the hope that "the human will may have time to understand itself". Also, Schopenhauer's phrase "the will to live" — designating the biological urge to survive and flourish which, according to him, actuates all living things — finds its way, as a key concept, into Santayana's *Rea-*

---

[2] Though not in fact for Schopenhauer. With regard to Schopenhauer's metaphysical doctrine (as briefly sketched in the essay 'Schopenhauer on the Basis of Morality'): he did not regard what is conventionally called ' the natural world' as the fundamental reality because that world was, in his view, only a version of reality: one constructed by human beings as a result of their subjective modes of apprehending the external world. It was, therefore, not reality as it was in itself, independent of human subjectivity. A succinct way of differentiating between Schopenhauer's and Santayana's positions is to say that the latter regards reality as being basically a physical order, and one describable by the science of physics, while the former sees reality as basically a *meta*physical order, not describable by physics.

[3] Though not, it should be remembered, in the metaphysical sense.

son in Religion, in the words, "In order to give the will to live frank and direct satisfaction ..."[b]

A further echo of Schopenhauer is found in the contrast the German philosopher draws between, on the one hand, willing and, on the other, will-free contemplation. The latter, for Schopenhauer, is the truly philosophical state. This state is characterised by Santayana in very similar terms when he says that philosophical investigation terminates in "a steady contemplation of all things in their order and worth." Also, for the philosopher, contemplation is "his only possible life ... He lives by thinking ..."[c] These words parallel what Schopenhauer says on the intellectual genius: "as knowledge and thought form a mode of activity natural and easy to him, he will also delight himself in them at all times...and so his mind will have no further aim than to be constantly active."[d]

For both men, moreover, the philosopher and the genius, by virtue of the qualities specified above, are to be sharply distinguished from the majority of human beings: who are, by definition, average and mediocre. It will be recalled that, in the essay 'The Protest Perspective and Meritocracy', I noted that Santayana embraces Schopenhauer's phrase for the majority: 'Fabrikwaaren der Natur'; this point needs only brief re-iteration now.

In general cultural outlook, both philosophers are global. This fact is all the more impressive in Schopenhauer's case, because in his day most Western thinkers were very Euro-centric. He, by contrast, was widely versed in Asian culture as well as Western: which of course partly explains his erudition in world religion. In both the religious and general philosophical context, he is especially interested in Indian thought. He regards Buddhism and Hinduism as the most philosophically respectable of all the world religions. Further, he sees fundamental ethical links between them and early Christianity:

> The New Testament ... must be in some way traceable to an Indian source: its ethical system, its ascetic view of morality, its pessimism and its Avatar, are all thoroughly Indian ... Everything which is true in Christianity may also be found in Brahmanism and Buddhism.[e]

Likewise, Santayana has a very high regard for the ethical aspects of Indian religion. Perhaps taking his lead from Schopenhauer, he too sees moral linkage between Buddhism and Christianity; he speaks of the "ascetic and quasi-Buddhistic element in Christianity".[f] In addition, Buddhism is praised because it "has kept morality pure—free from that admixture of worldly and partisan precepts with which less pessimistic systems are encumbered".[g]

A global outlook, yielding as it does a highly complex and relativistic view of human culture and experience, led both philosophers to spurn views of history based on the notion of inevitable progress, especially those views which focussed on the history of the West. With Schopenhauer: even if he had not been a cultural internationalist, his overall pessimism would have led him to reject Western-centred doctrines of progress, based on the concept of 'laws of history'. It would of course have led him to reject all such doctrines, whatever their geographical focus. Such rejection was a major part of his work in general. Representative of his anti-progressivism is the following: "A real philosophy of history can ... not consist in raising the temporal aims of man to the rank of absolutes, and furthermore, in constructing in an artificial and fanciful manner man's progress."[h]

Now, with Santayana: it will be remembered that the essay 'Russell and Santayana' contains a quotation articulating his disbelief in 'laws of history' (progressive or otherwise). To that quotation can be added these words attacking the idea of historicist providentialism —the view that history unfolds according to a providential (usually divinely-instigated) plan:

> whatever plausibility the providential view of a given occurrence may have is dependent on the curious limitation and selfishness of the observer's estimations ... all victors perish in their turn and everything, if you look far enough, falls back into the inexorable vortex.[i]

However, the above-stated similarities between Schopenhauer's and Santayana's perspectives on history, along with the other concurrences between them as specified in this essay, should not lead to the conclusion that their outlooks harmonised in every way. Indeed, we have already noted one important difference: Santayana's naturalistic position as against Schopenhauer's metaphysical one. There are other divergences as well, but, in concluding this essay, I wish to focus on just one: fundamental attitude to the world and human behaviour.

Schopenhauer's pervasive pessimism has previously been emphasised. Also, it has been noted, in the essay 'Santayana and Hardy', that Santayana evinced a melancholy tendency. At first, then, it might seem that there is little attitudinal difference between the two men. However, taking Santayana's work as a whole, we see that there is actually a big difference. Despite certain variations in mood, the essential thrust of his writing on ethical issues is that the human will *should* assert itself, though only in ways which are morally, socially and culturally constructive. His point is evident in the extended quotation from *Interpretations of Poetry and Religion* which was given at the end of the essay 'What is Ethical Rationality?' Santayana, writing emphatically in a post-Darwinian context, sees man as an animal naturally endowed with propulsive energy and will, and regards the latter as forces which ethics should serve.

Diametrically opposed to this is Schopenhauer's view of ethics. As briefly indicated in the essay 'Schopenhauer on the Basis of Morality', for him the ultimate goal of morality is to eradicate willing, not to serve it. Willing is the source of all suffering; therefore the final aim of ethics is deliverance from willing and suffering. By contrast: while Santayana of course recognises the large amount of suffering in human life — a recognition which secures him against historicist progressivism and social utopianism — he nevertheless regards the human will as, to repeat, deserving of positive considerations.

A further, related divergence: for Schopenhauer, the natural world[4] is something horrendous: "everywhere in nature we see contest, struggle and the fluctuation of victory ... This universal conflict is to be seen most clearly in the animal kingdom. Animals have the vegetable kingdom for their nourishment, and within the animal kingdom again, every animal is the prey of some other."[j] Conversely, while Santayana acknowledges the harsher aspects of the natural world, his overall view of nature is that it is, to a very large extent, a source of fascination and wonder. As regards nature's mechanical processes, he voices "delight in a mechanism that can fall into so many marvellous and beautiful shapes".[k] Moreover, he speaks of "this wonderful world".[l]

For that last phrase, or any equivalent to it, one will search in vain throughout the entire length and breadth of Schopenhauer's writings.

End Notes

[a] For Santayana, see in particular *Reason in Science*, p. 3. For Schopenhauer, see especially : "the day ... will soon come when religions will depart from European man like a nurse whose care the child has outgrown ..." In *Arthur Schopenhauer: Essays and Aphorisms* (Penguin Bks., 1970), p. 109.

[b] *Reason in Religion* (New York: Dover Publications, 1982 (1905)), p. 251.

---

[4] Understood by him, again, as a human-subjective way of apprehending the objective reality.

[c] Both quotations as given by Timothy Sprigge in *Santayana* (London and New York: Routledge, 1995 (1974)), pp. 7–8
[d] In *The Essential Schopenhauer* (London: Unwin Books, 1962), p. 75.
[e] *Ibid.*, pp. 24–5.
[f] *Reason in Science*, p. 230.
[g] *Ibid.*, p. 293.
[h] As quoted by Eric Heller in *The Disinherited Mind* (Penguin Bks., 1961 (1952)), p. 67.
[i] *Reason in Science*, p. 56.
[j] *The World as Will and Representation, Vol. 1*, trans. E.F.J. Payne (New York: Dover Publications Inc., 1958), pp. 146–7.
[k] *Reason in Science*, p. 90.
[l] *The Wisdom of Santayana*, p. 257.

Mill and Nietzsche

In terms of their traditional popular images, these two philosophers seem poles apart. In this corner, we have Mill, the measured English spokesman for liberal individualism, social fluidity, women's rights, and intelligent consideration of democracy and even socialism; someone extensively engaged in the radical social developments of the mid nineteenth century. While in the other corner, we have Nietzsche, also of the nineteenth century, but displaying an atavistic Teutonic emphasis on heroes and forceful action; someone hostile to radicalism, democracy, socialism, feminism, and favouring aristocratic forms of social organisation.

However, in both cases the traditional image requires some modification.[1] While a good deal of the content remains valid, a close reading of Mill and Nietzsche actually reveals a seminal similarity between them: both vigorously championed exceptional individuality, and saw its integrity as threatened by the tendency toward standardisation and uniformity which nineteenth century Western society was evincing. Such championship, in Mill's case, was consonant with his advocacy of liberal individualism and women's rights, but involved a highly qualified (while not hostile) attitude toward the growth of democratic culture and toward socialist thought. In fact, it led him to draw a generic distinction between what he called "persons of genius" and "the general average of mankind". This distinction brings him in line with Nietzsche, who has always been known for his ringing assertion of the value of genius as against mass-averageness. Moreover, it brings him in line with a power of emphasis which needs to be fully appreciated.

The vigour of Mill's support for the exceptional individual, and of his critique of averageness, is conveyed unequivocally in the following two extracts from *On Liberty* (1859):

> *Persons of genius* ... are, and are always likely to be, a small minority; but in order to preserve them, it is necessary to preserve the

---

[1] In Nietzsche's case, of course, the modification has long been under way, especially in Anglo-American culture over the last half century. The complexity, subtlety and multifariousness of Nietzsche's work have been increasingly recognised — and, it must be added, acknowledged as co-existing with other elements in his work which are morally dubious or even repugnant.

soil in which they grow ... Persons of genius are ... more individual than any other people ... I insist thus emphatically on the importance of genius, and the necessity of allowing it to unfold itself freely both in thought and practice ... but knowing also that almost everyone,in reality, is totally indifferent to it ... nearly all, at heart, think they can do very well without it ... *Originality* is the one thing which *unoriginal minds* cannot feel the use of ... whatever homage may be professed, or even paid, to real or supposed mental superiority, the general tendency of things throughout the world is to render *mediocrity* the ascendant power among mankind ... Those whose opinions go by the name of public opinion ... are always a *mass* ... collective mediocrity ... The honour and glory of the *average man* is that ... he can respond internally to wise and noble things [as created or discovered by exceptional individuals] (Italics mine)[a]

And:

The general average of mankind are not only moderate in intellect, but also moderate in inclinations: they have no tastes or wishes strong enough to incline them to do anything unusual, and they consequently do not understand those who have ... [The public's] ideal of character is to be without any marked character; to maim ... every part of human nature which stands out prominently and tends to make the person markedly dissimilar in outline to *commonplace humanity.* (Italics mine.)[b]

Now, compare these words with those of Nietzsche on the broad theme of difference between exception and average:

If one knows how to keep the exceptions principally in view, I mean the greatly gifted and pure of soul ... one may believe in the value of life, because then one is *overlooking* all other men ... And likewise if ... one accords validity only to *one* species of drives, the less egotistical, and justifies them in the face of all others, then one can again hope for something of mankind as a whole and to this extent believe in the value of life ... [But] The great majority endure life without complaining overmuch; they *believe* in the value of existence, but they do so precisely because each of them exists for himself alone, refusing to step outside of himself as those exceptions do: everything outside themselves they notice not at all or at most as a dim shadow. Thus for the ordinary, everyday man, the value of life rests solely on the fact that he regards himself more highly than he does the world. The great lack of imagination from which he suffers means he is unable to feel his way into other beings and thus he participates as little as possible in their fortunes and sufferings.[c, 2]

Also:

Assuming now that need has always brought only those people together who could express similar needs and experiences with similar symbols, then we shall find, all things considered, that this easy *communicability* of need, which means ultimately the experiencing of merely average and common experiences, must have been the most powerful of all the forces which have ever ruled mankind... One must call upon enormous oppositional powers in order to contend against this natural, all too natural *progressus in simile*, the continuous progress of man toward similarity, ordinariness, the average ... [d]

Setting the Mill and Nietzsche extracts side by side, it cannot be said that the latter outdo the former in terms of robust outspokenness, a quality for which Nietzsche is customarily renowned. In fact, there is a case for saying that Mill has the edge in this respect.

Regarding Mill's attitude to socialism in the light of his words on outstanding individuality: his reservations about democratic culture as foregrounding the average and mediocre led him to argue that socialism could not completely look to democratic values for the political leadership it would require, at least in its initial phase. Leaders would have to be morally exceptional, because they would be taking on enormous responsibility for only very little in the way of financial remuneration and conventional social status. This conception of leadership, though in the context of socialism, is not far removed from that delineated, at various points in his work, by Nietzsche, the anti-socialist, on moral and intellectual aristocracy in politics.

On women, there can be no denying that Nietzsche frequently, perhaps predominantly, expressed negative views, even if these were sometimes subtle and witty rather than harshly disparaging. Nevertheless, on certain occasions his estimate was highly positive. A major example of this is when he conveys his conception of a good marriage: "Marriage: that I call the will of two to create the one who is more than those two who created it. Reverence before one another,

---

[2] Note, incidentally, that here Nietzsche defines the exceptional individual as one who is "less egotistical", and more sympathetic to others, than are the majority. This definition is very close to that of Schopenhauer. When writing these words, Nietzsche was still deeply influenced by Schopenhauer.

as before the willers of such a will — that I call marriage. Let this be the meaning and truth of your marriage."[e]

Note how the woman is addressed as equal to the man: as of the same standing in marital contribution and creativity, and as equally deserving of respect. Indeed, the relationship envisaged here reminds us in many ways of the real-life one between Mill and Harriet Taylor: one whose keynote was mutual esteem and shared development. And Nietzsche goes even further than this in positive estimate of women when he avers: "the perfect woman is a higher type of humanity than the perfect man, and also something much rarer."[f] Here again, Nietzsche is very close to Mill.

Finally, returning to Mill's theme of liberal individualism, certain moments in Nietzsche's work definitely strike a liberal-individualist note — one, it must be added, very different to that sounded at other times in his writing. If the note in question is defined, at least in part, as a distancing from authoritarian attitudes and behaviour, as a valuing of privacy and inner mental development, and an eschewing of militancy, dogmatism and coerciveness, then this is certainly what we find in Nietzsche's delineation of what he regards as the true philosopher:

> They [philosophers] think of the things they cannot do without: freedom from constraint, interference ... a clear head, the free, joyous play of the mind ... no pangs of frustrated ambition ... a heart turned to the future ... [Philosophers seek] A deliberate obscurity; a side-stepping of fame; a backing-away from noise, adulation, accolades, influence; a modest position, a quotidian existence, something that hides more than it reveals ... For philosophers need peace above all ... We reverence all that is quiet, cold, distinguished ... a mind sure of itself speaks quietly, seeks out hidden places, is in no hurry. It is easy to tell a philosopher.[g]

Mill would have completely concurred with the mellowness and non-aggressiveness of this image, and perhaps only taken exception to its implied absence of significant social participation.

End Notes

[a]   *On Liberty*, pp. 74–6.
[b]   *Ibid.*, p. 79. The reader will recall that part of this quotation was previously given in the essay 'The Protest Perspective and Meritocracy'.
[c]   *Human, All Too Human,* trans. R.J. Hollingdale (Cambridge University Press, 1986 (1878)), p. 29.
[d]   *Beyond Good and Evil,* trans. Marianne Cowan (Chicago: Henry Regnery Company, 1955 (1886)), p. 217.

[e]   *Thus Spake Zarathustra* trans. R.J. Hollingdale (Penguin Bks. Ltd., 1961 (1883)), p. 95.
[f]   As quoted by Will Durant, *The Story of Philosophy*, p. 373.
[g]   *The Genealogy of Morals,* III, 8.

A Necessary Hardness

"The unexamined life is not worth living", declared Socrates, and with a terseness which remains effective despite the passage of nearly two and a half thousand years since the words were spoken. In addition of course to the manner of delivery, the actual content of what is delivered retains major impact, and for a number of important reasons.

Let's begin by pointing out that the phrase "The unexamined life" entails two possible interpretations. One is that the life in question is one that could have been examined by the person living it, but wasn't. The other is that the life could not have been examined by the person concerned, due to lack of mental capacity. I wish to focus on this second interpretation.

This focus, I should specify, is in the context of a general outlook which is secularist and humanistic. This is a pivotal point because Socrates's statement is a human appraisal of a human life, and one which carries finality. Though Socrates himself was not, in any strictly modern sense, a secularist or humanist, he was in fact doing what secularists and humanists do: making an evaluative judgement about a human being which is regarded as absolute in the sense of not being subject to modification or refutation by any supra-human mode of judgement i.e. a divine mode. The secular view is that human judgement is not subject to such a mode because, simply, the latter does not exist. Human appraisal is final because there is none superior to it — indeed, none other than it.

For those who concur that human evaluation possesses conclusive status, attention centres on the problem of mental incapacity, as referred to previously. This problem is inevitably connected with issues raised by eugenic arguments. It also links with issues to do with social and environmental resources, and with the complexity of the modern scientific world-view.

In relation to all these areas of concern, let us consider the case of someone who, for genetic or other pre-natal reasons, is utterly incapable of self-knowledge and intelligent self-direction. This person's life will be seen, by all who accept the Socratic criterion, as not worth living. Further, from a eugenic standpoint, the position will be that measures to prevent the birth of such extreme defectiveness should be strongly advocated, and for two chief reasons. Firstly, these measures will preclude the mental suffering which the extreme defective may well bring upon himself and on those closest to him. Secondly, they will rule out the possibility of his passing on his defective genes to others, and so carrying forward an insoluble problem to the next generation. Foremost among such measures should be counselling and advice to prospective parents, based on the technology of genetic screening, a technology whose development should be invested in to the maximal possible extent.

Such an approach may seem hard, but, if the arguments stated above and to come later are sound, then this hardness is necessary: it is inescapably called for by the biological situation.

Having briefly considered the broad eugenic perspective, let's move on to the issue of social and economic resources. The provisions required for the life-long care of extreme defectives are supplied without any counter-balancing factor. The recipients of those resources cannot reciprocate, either in terms of constructive, useful activities or financial earnings. It is true that, in affluent societies, this non-reciprocation is not a big problem, since provisions can be supplied without any major strain on the economy. (Such, at any rate, is the case while the incidence of extreme defectiveness remains small.) However, in non-affluent societies, provision can put huge pressure on the economy—indeed, the society may be able to provide hardly any resources at all. In situations like this, the basic problem of defectiveness increases in grimness, especially given the fact that impoverished societies cannot afford the screening technology needed in the first place for reducing the number of births of defectives.

Finally, let's look at the considerations bound up with the complexity of the scientific world-view. Arguably, these are less pressing than those linked with the issue of resources; but, if viewed in a sufficiently wide perspective, emerge as very important indeed. For the secular humanist, empirical science has opened up a view of reality so vast and challenging in its myriad-details, and at the same time so suggestive of how much is as yet unknown, that religious ontologies appear pathetically diminutive and quaintly anthropomorphic by comparison. The scientific vision is an intellectual inheritance of such stupendous proportions that human dignity and courage expand in the embracing of it. But the embracing of it, or at least the attempt to do so, requires advanced powers of mind, combined with unflagging intellectual scrupulousness and dedication.

Massive cognition of reality is therefore a rare attainment, and one always conscious of its boundaries. At considerable distance below it lies average intellectual performance, and that distance is a source of regret to those capable of perceiving it. Deeper still is the regret at the larger distance where performance just below the average is located. But deepest of all is the regret at the huge distance separating the rare level of perception from the feeble line of sight found in the extreme defective. To be permanently ignorant of self, and therefore forever unable to come to terms with one's existence, is to be cut off from the very minimum of significant knowledge, let alone from the vast dimensions lying beyond that minimum. And to be incapable of intelligent self-direction is to forever unable to evaluate one's actions, learn from experience, forge a life-path. Would it not be better, one is prompted to ask, to take measures to avoid the unrelievable powerlessness of such a predicament? In the pre-natal context, eugenics offers an answer to this question, an answer outlined previously; and one which is, in the nature of the case, necessarily austere.

Secularism as Against Religion

Introductory text for Debate at University of East London, 13.9.08.

In arguing for secularism as against religion, I should begin by defining the terms I am using. My dictionary's definition of the 'secularist' is: "one who rejects every form of religious faith and every kind of religious worship". Also, the adjective 'secular' is defined as: "pertaining to this present world or to things not spiritual or sacred: disassociated with religious teaching or religious use". If the terms 'spiritual' and 'sacred' are understood as meaning 'not part of the present or natural world,' then all the above words convey the essential features of my own position.

Now let's look at what is said about the word 'religion': "the feeling of reverence which people entertain toward a god; the recognition of God as an object of worship, love and obedience; piety; any system of faith and worship." In turn, the adjective 'religious' is characterized as: "pertaining or relating to religion ... imbued with religion ... devoted by vows to the practice of religion ..." These words convey the very opposite of my own position.

Given the above definitions of religion, it should immediately be pointed out that not all systems of faith involve belief in deity. Most do, but there are exceptions, Buddhism being the leading example. So perhaps the key point to make about all religions, theistic and otherwise, is that they all rest on *faith* of some kind. (In Buddhism, incidentally, belief in metempsychosis is a matter of faith.)

This reliance on faith is, from the secularist standpoint, a major problem. Secularists in general are oriented toward science and scientific philosophy. The latter can be defined as a mode of speculation about the structure of reality which constantly refers to scientific findings, and which never moves in directions independent of these findings. Such thinking, therefore, is always referenced to what is known, and most secularists regard scientific knowledge as the only objective form of knowledge. Clearly, then, faith-based systems of thought are antithetical to this outlook. They focus on what is not known, and what therefore must be believed in. Faith, by definition, is to do with the unknown.

A closely related problem is that, with most religions, the supreme object of faith is a deity who is said to be situated outside the natural world i.e. is *super*natural in character.[1] The supernaturalistic view of deity obviously widens the gap with secularism, given the latter's predominant commitment to science. Secularists will inevitably ask how, exactly, the supernatural is to be defined. Even if a definition is provided, the matter must end there as regards scientific investigation, since the supernatural, as an object of faith rather than of knowledge, must be assumed to be outside the sphere of science. This is unlike definitions of entities in the natural world, because these definitions can be extensively supplemented by scientific data. The doctrine of naturalism, in contrast to that of supernaturalism, can be broadly characterized as the view that every aspect of reality is, in principle if not always in practice, accessible to scientific investigation; and most secularists, in rejecting notions of the supernatural, see the investigative role of science as potentially limitless.

Of course, the supernaturalist may retort that his deity is actually not an object of faith but of knowledge. But if so, he is then faced with the question of the *mode* of knowledge in question. If the mode is not scientific, and not derived from investigation and experimentation, then what kind is it? Also, how can that knowledge be conveyed to others? It will not do, incidentally, to argue that the mode of knowledge is intuitive, and can be conveyed by appealing to the intuition of others. That line of argument begs far too many questions.

The emphasis placed by secularists on science is due not only to a deep respect for the various scientific disciplines, and for the methods they adopt to verify, or falsify, postulates made about the structure of reality. It derives also from moral, social and political considerations. When there is a conflict of viewpoint between social groups, it can be of a scientific or a faith nature. If the former, attempts can be made to resolve it by deploying the standard scientific procedures of, to repeat, investigation and experimentation. Further, it's important to point out that these procedures obtain throughout the world scientific community: they are universal. Genuine science has a shared set or range of methods, constituting a sin-

---

[1] It's true that not all deities are regarded as supernatural. Pantheists, for example, see their god and the natural world as being identical. But pantheism is the exception among theistic religions—and is especially at odds with the theisms of Judaism, Christianity and Islam.

gle methodology, not different methodologies split along sectarian lines. By contrast, if the dispute is faith-based, no common procedure for resolution is or can be available. This fact is more likely to lead to hostility and even violence between disputants than when the conflict is of a scientific nature. Such is evidenced by the number of wars of religion with which history—both of West and East—is scarred. So far, there have been no wars of science.

In general, the scientific mindset is less inclined to hostile and violent attitudes because it is not dogmatic: it does base itself on rigid, unchangeable positions. Of the essence of true science is a careful and tentative approach in making knowledge-claims, plus a continual readiness to revise, amend or abandon a position when new knowledge comes to light, and to listen attentively to counter-claims and alternative interpretations. Far less of this open-mindedness and flexibility is displayed by most religious institutions, which rely heavily on dogma.

In allying himself to science, the secularist is of course aware that dogmatism is not confined to religion. Certain non-religious ways of thinking also display it: for example, the Stalinist version of Marxism in the former Soviet Union, and the Pol Pot version of Marxism in Cambodia in the 1970s. However, it is quite clear that neither of these doctrines was genuinely scientific. They were extremely dogmatic, though the dogmas were obviously not of a supernaturalistic kind. It is only in the sense that they were not supernaturalistic that the doctrines can be called secular. In all other respects, they have no relation to the secularism I have been discussing, which opposes dogmatism of all kinds.

Further points to be made about the linkage between secularism and moral issues are as follows: One of the criticisms frequently made of secularism by religious institutions is that it lacks moral certainty. To this charge, most secularists must in fact plead guilty. But that is only because the majority of secularists do not think that ethical certainty—meaning certainty about what is right and wrong and therefore about what values to hold—is actually attainable. They generally argue that the entire notion of moral certainty is usually bound up with religious belief, specifically with the view that a deity exists who holds certain ethical values and has transmitted these to mankind, for the latter to follow.[2] If, by contrast, there is no belief in

---

[2] About this view, in passing, the question needs to be asked: does the deity promulgate these values because they are his own, or because they are valid

deity, then this whole way of viewing morality has to be jettisoned. The main secularist position is that ethical systems have evolved as part of man's general social and cultural history. The many differences between the moral codes of the past and present, and also between those existing at present, are due to a huge range of social and cultural variables. Moreover, those elements which most or all moral systems do actually share reflect certain psychic features common to the entire human species as it has evolved physically. Hence, ethics is viewed in a naturalistic, historical and relativistic way. Concepts of divine revelation and command, ones which of course entail moral certainty, are no part of this perspective.

Lack of ethical certainty is not seen by secularists as a weakness, just as lack of factual certainty in the sciences is not seen as such. On the contrary, uncertainty is regarded as an inevitable consequence of the naturalistic perspective defined above, and one to be honestly and openly acknowledged. There are no revelations to be had, no intuitions or inspired insights to be experienced; and it is on arguments which claim the contrary that the burden of proof lies. In the absence of revelation and discovery, secularists readily admit that moral issues are deeply problematic and highly complex.

Yet, in the midst of this complexity, they do have some clear lines of approach. They hold to certain basic humanitarian values: those of sensitivity, tolerance, respect, and of course love. These values are seen as totally naturalistic in character; also, no claim is made that they represent or reflect any objective discovery of what is right and wrong. Secularists are of course prepared to argue for them, but the terms of the argument involve no reference to, again, divinity or revelation. Within these restrained and non-dogmatic parameters of discourse, secularists do in fact pursue large-scale moral goals: the maximizing of human flourishing and wellbeing, which includes the maximizing of fruitful and constructive relations between groups and individuals; and the consequent minimising of suffering and conflict.

Finally, despite the many oppositions between the secularist and the religious outlook, it's worth noting that many secularists are far from unsympathetic to everything in religious culture. Their view is that, from an historical standpoint, religious culture was the first sustained attempt to meet the two most fundamental needs of the human psyche: to achieve an organized morality and to construct a

---

independently of the fact that they are his own? If the latter, a further question is raised: does the source of morality actually lie outside deity?

general picture of reality. Religion, then, has made contributions to ethical and ontological thinking which are of major interest. This is the case even though religion's ontological efforts were completely pre-scientific. And more: the ethical thinking of the leading figures in the world religions has indisputably sounded the depths of the human heart. But the *human* heart: secularism insists that everything that is significant in religion is so because it serves as an index of the profundities of which human beings are capable. Hence many of the most important things in religious culture are on a par with great art—indeed, *are* great art: no secularist would deny the enormous artistic creativity which religion has fostered, in literature, music, painting, architecture and many other spheres. In these ways, religion has historically been perhaps the main conduit for human expressiveness. However, once again, emphasis must fall on the final adjective in the statement.

This humanistic perspective on religion has, clearly, much positive content. Nonetheless, secularism keeps to its view that ethical and ontological thinking must abandon their traditional reliance on religious doctrines, in the effort to maximize the freedom of thought which is indispensable for the achievement of both full human co-operation and a true picture of the universe.

Various

Science and Comradeship: We could perhaps define the psychological need which religions have traditionally sought to satisfy as the need to attain the most capacious, the most emotionally inclusive, mode of response to one's fellow human beings. This need is perennial; and, with the decline of supernaturalistic religious doctrines, it must now be met in ways which (in contrast to most religions) do not clash with the scientific perspective. One route to achieving that deepest response-level is social and political—provided the latter is free of anti-scientific ways of thinking i.e. dogmatism. In fact, in a culture which is genuinely scientific, the social and political is a main route, since it can share with science a complete independence of belief in the supernatural. Hence, once social co-operation has been chosen, science can nourish and reinforce that commitment, supplying—as science itself develops—an ever-expanding means to attain ends. In this way, science can be integral to the achievement of the profoundest mutuality and comradeship through social action.

. . .

Instead of rigid ideology: "The age of political ideology is over", say so many people. And yes, it is over, if by 'ideology' is meant rigid doctrines which claim to have the answer to every social question, and which are therefore utopianist. Such a way of thinking about political and social issues is, as far as genuine and realistic intellectual activity is concerned, definitely a thing of the past. But this does not mean that all forms of generalized, principled and panoramic ways of thinking about politics have become invalid. A crucial distinction must be drawn between doctrinairism and other large-scale approaches to politics which are truly empirical, therefore flexible, cognizant of complexity, and self-revising. An empirically synoptic approach means combining the following: moral commitment with critical alertness; the aim of ameliorating social conditions with careful consideration of actions which might, unintentionally, work against that aim; a sense of what is feasibly achievable with a sense of what is not.

Such an approach, which can be described as activism containing a critical perspective, regards effort at betterment as on-going, indeed never-ending. Hence it is extremely dubious of the notion of 'the end of history', which alleges that a time will come when endeavours at large-scale improvement will no longer be necessary.

Central to this approach is a focus on the problem of the kinds of economic and political power which are democratically unaccountable. Actuating principles are either to make that power accountable or, if the common good requires, to dismantle it. Struggle against self-interested power elites is probably perennial. So too is that against power elites who do not regard themselves as self-interested and who adhere to an ideology which they think justifies their possessing power — but who are, nevertheless, in practice autocratic and undemocratic.[1] Such struggle holds central position in the kind of activism previously defined, and has in fact been central to progressive endeavour throughout history. That it will remain so is a probability sufficiently strong to undermine the 'end of history' thesis.

· · ·

Moral Attachment. Active attachment to the great, perennial moral issues is one of the things most likely to alleviate personal loneliness. This attachment can be broadly social, or specifically political, or both. Increasingly, with the decline of supernaturalistic religious doctrines as loci of involvement, it will be seen as the most viable form of large-scale ethical engagement with others. Without it, the demise of supernaturalistic outlooks inevitably produces a sense of isolation in the people who previously depended on them; but with it, that sense can be avoided, for these people and for everyone else. This attachment is a mode of self-transcendence: but of course a naturalistic mode, whose perspective, sphere of reference and goals are not super-human but universally human.

· · ·

Laws of Physics: 'Laws' of physics are *words* or *concepts* referring to the regular behaviours of physical objects: or, more precisely, to the regular behaviours experienced thus far. However, the term 'physical object' can also be applied to the behaviours themselves. Thus it can denote both a physical object and its activities. So, returning to our first point, 'laws' can refer to physical objects in both the above senses. But, since they do no more than refer to or denote, 'laws' are not themselves physical objects. They are therefore not physical *things* controlling other physical things.

---

[1] These points about elites are especially relevant to issues surrounding the possibility that the global balance of economic and therefore political power may shift from West to East.

· · ·

Existents can only be described: To the question, "Why are there existents, rather than total non-existence?" no viable answer can be given. The answer cannot be of the form, "Because such-and-such exists as causal factor," since anything that exists is, by definition, part of the *question,* not of the answer. And there is no other meaningful form the answer can take. The question being unanswerable, all that science and ontology can do is *describe*: convey the facts about the entities and processes that exist and have existed. Thus the only further objective knowledge which humanity can hope to possess is further attainments in accurate description of existents. Existence is a sphere to be charted, not accounted for.

· · ·

(The following should be read with reference to the earlier essay, 'What is Ethical Rationality?')

Are there value-facts? The argument that 'value-facts' exist is bound up with the view that virtue — what is morally good — can be factually cognized. Hence the position is that of ethical cognitivism, objectivism, realism: moral values are objects of discovery and knowledge.

Ethical cognitivism usually takes the form of contending that virtues are located both within the human mind, as internal objects of moral knowledge, and outside the mind, as external objects of such knowledge. Hence the mind, working from an internal perception of virtue, applies that perception to the behaviours it sees in the external world. These behaviours, as objects of moral perception, can be *factually described* as virtuous, in just the same way that a table can be factually described as wooden. Thus the vocabulary of ethical cognitivism consists only of fact-terms, and contains no value-terms. 'Virtuous' is as much a fact-term as 'wooden'.

According to this argument, behaviours objectively possess moral qualities, and do so in an independent, autonomous way. So, actions never become virtuous by having moral qualities conferred or bestowed on them by the outlook of the person or group observing them. They already contain these qualities, as in-built, intrinsic characteristics; and ones that can be readily cognized. Also, because cognitivist discourse deals only in fact-terms, there is *only* factual description of the moral qualities in behaviour, never an expression of opinion about those qualities: never, therefore, evaluation, appraisal or judgement of them.

Clearly, ethical cognitivism and the argument for value-facts stand in diametric opposition to the reasoning of ethical non-cognitivism. According to the latter, moral qualities *are* conferred on actions by the mind of the observer, by the moral outlook. Behaviours have no in-built moral characteristics. The latter are bestowed on them by acts of moral appraisal. To use Hume's metaphor, the appraiser "guilds" the action with his evaluation of it. Speaking more broadly, appraisal-communities (moral cultures) guild the action with their judgement of it. The analogy (again from Hume) is with optics, where the observer, by a complex optical process, invests an external object with 'colour': something which does not actually exist in the object itself.

By fully and openly acknowledging the above appraisal-process, ethical non-cognitivism foregoes any claim to possessing objective knowledge of good and evil. 'Good' and 'evil' are not qualities discovered in behaviour but qualities applied to it.

This perspective clearly separates facts from values. The fact is the behaviour itself. The value is something applied to the latter. Hence it is possible to refer to an action in three quite distinct verbal modes. One mode is exclusively factual, physically descriptive, and devoid of value-terms. It can be used no matter how appalling, from a *moral* standpoint, the action may be deemed. (This mode is different from the one deployed by moral cognitivism, as referred to previously, where words which are arguably value-terms, such as 'virtuous,' are presented as fact-terms. In this mode, the language is non-controversially factual.) The second mode is a mixture of fact-terms and value-terms. The third is only value-terms. That all three modes can be deployed shows that the sphere of fact can be clearly separated from that of value: while values are facts in the sense that they exist (in minds), value-*outlooks* are not knowledge-outlooks, therefore not factual outlooks.

Overall, the non-cognitivist position is far more reflective of the complexity of moral issues than is the cognitivist. One is bound to ask: if moral values can be discovered and indisputably known, why has there been so much variation in moral perspectives throughout human history, and why is there so much now? Surely, once something is discovered and becomes an indisputable object of knowledge, it remains so. Thus, if genuine moral discoveries had been made by specific groups at specific times, they would have been endorsed, swiftly or gradually, by the rest of humanity. If gradually, then this process would perhaps still be going on today. That such is definitely *not* true either of the past or the present suggests that moral discourse is very different from that of science, where real discoveries are made and are cumulatively acknowledged. Non-cognitivism, in never claiming to make discoveries or be scientific, avoids the moral dogmatism that is endemic in the cognitivist outlook. Also, we should note that its non-dogmatism extends to those aspects of past and present moral perspectives where there *is* agreement and harmony, or at least a large measure of it. Such harmony, it argues, is not a sign that discoveries have been made, but probably indicates certain universal characteristics in the human species, incurred as the latter has evolved biologically, and manifesting themselves in all different kinds of cultural context. Finally, its non-dogmatism provides a basis for the flexible and mutually responsive form of moral dialogue which is the best hope for achieving and maintaining global peace.

· · ·

Ethical Consequentialism. Though this position is based on the view that actions should be morally judged according to their consequences, the implication is *not* that ethical values are in any way dependent on those consequences. Clearly, if values are being applied to consequences as a way of appraising the latter, they must be independent of, and anterior to, the latter. The values do not arise from the consequences. If they did, there would be no way of judging the latter; grounds for appraisal must be external, not internal, to objects of appraisal.

However, this anteriority of values does not mean that the latter have to be seen as cognitive i.e. as forms of discovery, as perceptions of what is right and wrong—which is how moral cognitivists view values. On the contrary, values can justifiably be regarded as non-cognitive i.e not forms of knowledge of right and wrong, hence subjective or inter-subjective. As such, they are still prior to the consequences to which they are applied.

Comte's Continuing Relevance

Amended text, reproduced by kind permission of 'Imprint Academic'.

Auguste Comte was born in 1798 and died in 1857. Though much in his writings is now dated, he remains a seminal figure in a number of respects. Firstly, he defined, as clearly as anyone has in the last 200 years, the pivotal and transformational role of science in the modern world. Next, despite this emphasis on the crucial importance of science, he rightly insisted that the purposes for which we utilise science can never be derived from science itself . That is to say, those purposes are affective and pre-rational in character. Thirdly, as a related point, he made an important contribution to the theory that human behaviour displays certain perennial and universal features, and that, in this sense, there is a human nature. Finally, as someone who regarded the supernaturalistic doctrines of religion as doomed, to be replaced by science, he advocated a particular form of humanism which many people find both realistic and satisfying.

However, before going on to look at these topics in some detail, let us, in the interests of balance, briefly say more about those aspects of Comte's work which are now outmoded. To begin with, he shared with Durkheim and Herbert Spencer a far too optimistic view of industrial capitalism, and wrongly assumed that this system, in contrast to feudalism, tended toward peace rather than war. Here, Marx, with his acute sense of the sectional and class interests at work in capitalism, was much more insightful about the system's capacity for conflict and aggression.[1] It was not that Comte failed to perceive class interests. In fact, he openly acknowledged that the capitalist system was and always would be controlled by those who were the wealthiest and most powerful. But he thought that this ruling class could be induced to exercise its power in ways which materially benefitted the whole of society as well as itself, thereby creating a harmony of economic interests.

---

[1]   A capacity on full display, of course, in the twentieth century.

As to how the ruling class could be so induced, Comte argued that the agency could and should be groups of scientists and philosophers: people of intellectual profundity and high moral calibre, who were also economically disinterested. They would constitute a kind of moral order whose function would be to temper and limit the power of those who headed the economic order, and to give the latter moral guidance. However, once again, Comte can be charged with a gross lack of realism. As Marx and others would have asked: How exactly is the spiritual order to affect the economic? What effective power could the spiritual order impose on the economic if the latter simply refused to listen? These are questions perhaps too obvious to need stating, and ones rendered inevitable by the harsh experience of economic/political power since Comte's day; yet they are ones which Comte himself overlooked.

The criticisms which can be made of Comte on this score do not necessarily mean that all notions of a moral sphere which is distinct from the economic are invalid. For example, Emile Durkheim had a number of interesting ideas on the same subject.[2] But it is clear that cogent thinking on this topic must include considerations of political and executive power. When it does, such thinking can be very significant indeed.

As regards Comte's views on science: while he rightly saw scientific development as the distinctive characteristic of the modern world, his overall view of science was, by contemporary standards, limited. For him, science was not an endless exploration of reality, an activity in which positions and perspectives were constantly being qualified, modified or amended. It was, on the contrary, a source of fixed and final certainties — indeed of dogma. His position was the classically Newtonian one that the formulation of a specific law is valid for all time, and not just for experience thus far. This view, which refuses to regard current formulations as only probably true in relation to the future, is emphatically pre-twentieth century.

Further, his conception of law in science was linked to one of law in history. Like Marx, though in a different frame of reference, he contended that there were laws of historical development; hence, that history travelled inexorably in a certain direction. Comte's frame of reference was one we shall soon examine in more detail: namely, an historical process by which mankind moved inevitably and totally from theological and metaphysical modes of thinking to

---

[2] As did Comte's nineteenth century contemporaries in England: Coleridge, Carlyle and Arnold.

one that was scientific and—because based on observation and direct experience—positivistic.

Comte's contention, asserting as it does the inevitable, complete and permanent triumph of the scientific over the non-scientific mindset, is clearly at variance with many anti-scientific tendencies in the contemporary world, especially the resurgence of religious fundamentalism and the continuing adherence to religion of a very large proportion of the world's population. The ultimate and global victory of the scientific outlook which Comte envisaged is, 150 years after his death, nowhere in sight: there are no indications of the historical inevitability of that triumph.

However, let us treat this point of criticism as a bridge to lead us back to positive commentary on Comte. We said at the beginning that he correctly identified the vital role of science in the modern world. As applied to the process of intellectual emancipation in Western Europe and North America in the nineteenth and twentieth centuries, Comte's point remains largely valid; likewise, as applied to the process of emancipation in other parts of the world. Science has unquestionably been the distinctive (though not only) agent of progress in the West and elsewhere over the last two centuries. This point needs of course to be qualified by the consideration that the effect of science on thought has been highly variable and remains so: that its influence on people has differed markedly in degree, depending on intellectual capacity, culture and environment. But even so, there can be no denying the fundamental changes it has produced. These changes make the intellectual history of the West since about 1800 qualitatively different from all preceding periods (though less so from the period 1700–1800 than from earlier centuries): a point which remains valid despite the persistence of various anti-scientific tendencies, as previously referred to.

Hence Comte was absolutely correct to draw a distinction between the predominantly scientific character of modern industrial society and the predominantly non-scientific character of pre-industrial, feudal society. In addition, he saw clearly that the scientist was largely replacing the ecclesiastic as society's source of ontological illumination (and now, at last, the illumination was genuine). Because, now, we do not normally look to religious bodies for factual instruction, we tend to forget that to do so was actually the norm in pre-scientific eras. Of this foundational change, we are forcefully reminded by reading Comte.

Let us now look in more detail at Comte's view of the intellectual history of mankind, a history which for him culminated in the attainment of the positivistic outlook. This history fell into three distinct phases. In the first, man tried to explain natural phenomena by attributing them to the actions of beings or forces like himself. This was the theological and animistic phase. In the second, phenomena were explained by reference, not to gods or spirits but to entities such as 'nature' or, in the case of Kant and Schopenhauer, to 'things-in-themselves'. This was the metaphysical phase. In the third and final phase, the one in which the most advanced minds were now located, man went no further than observing phenomena and perceiving regular links, laws, between them. He surrendered the notion, which had been characteristic of the theological and metaphysical stages, of a final principle or purpose lying behind observable facts, and was content to describe, in a purely empirical fashion, the workings of nature. This was the strictly scientific and positivistic phase.

Comte regarded the movement from one phase to another as inevitable because, as humanity's purview widened in thought and experience, the inadequacies of the theological and metaphysical viewpoints became increasingly obvious. Only the positivistic perspective could provide a full outlet for human enquiry. Hence positivism was man's ultimate intellectual position—indeed, his destiny.

Comte's argument is clearly reasonable, and the three modes of thought he delineates are the chief three of which we have historical knowledge (although Comte's chronology of modes must be subjected to close historical and anthropological analysis). At the same time, we have to add to criticisms that were made earlier. Comte under-estimated the power possessed by atavistic styles of thinking to stage come-backs—sometimes spectacular ones. Of this power, the afore-mentioned resurgence of religious fundamentalism is a recent example. In the West, that resurgence has been the most prominent in the United States, the country which also leads the world in science and technology. This shows that scientific advance provides no absolute guarantee against reversions to non-scientific or pre-scientific ways of thinking. A similar point can be made about Germany in the inter-war years: a country with a great scientific tradition which nevertheless succumbed to a primitive ideology. A further observation is that in many societies, science peacefully co-exists with religion of a non-fundamentalist, moderate and 'liberal' form. Overall, then, the picture is nowhere near as clear-cut as Comte thought. If it is true that mankind does move chronologically through the three intellectual stages, then this is the case only in a *partial* and *limited* sense. History shows no complete and irreversible transition from one phase to another. Hence there is no demonstrable law of total transition. The future is likely to evince, like past and present, a plurality of outlooks.

That said, what is of unquestionable importance for the secularist in Comte's outlook is his clear delineation of the positivistic mode of thinking. The movement from theology and metaphysics to positivism (including its more recent form, logical positivism) has essentially been a shift from a teleological to a mechanistic mode of explanation. In other words, positivism explains event-sequences only in terms of causal links between each event in the sequence, and not in terms of any pre-established purpose which the sequence as a whole is alleged to serve. Positivism embraces the concept of causal law, but does not equate law with purpose. Further, while Comte's notion of law was, as we have noted, Newtonian and too rigid, the notion of law is still of course a feature of science; only now — as has been previously said — current law-formulations are seen as only probably applicable to future experience.

In addition, positivism remains a key approach to understanding the structure of reality and its processes. This is the case despite the fact that it rests content with the notion that laws exist, and does not seek explanations for why these laws are as they are (thought to be) and not otherwise, or indeed for why any laws exist at all. While the attempt to achieve the latter kind of explanation (as made, for example, by Schopenhauer) is not to be dismissed as illegitimate, it is nevertheless less likely to produce an understanding of reality than is the positivist approach. This is so because the attempt ventures into dubious areas of speculation beyond the field of empirical science. The latter's goal is no more and no less than the correct ascertainment of what the laws are, and this goal is pursued by well-authenticated scientific methods. As part of empirical science, positivism shares these procedures, and is therefore a more reliable route to comprehending reality than are those attempts at understanding which seek to go beyond scientific method.

Moreover, though it is true that the positivistic mindset, bound up as it is with empiricism and what is generally accepted as scientific procedure, is neither universal nor likely to become so in the foreseeable future, still the secularist cannot help wishing it *were so*. It deserves to be. Hence secularists can look for sustenance to Comte as being, in a general way, one of the great nineteenth century advocates of science: albeit an advocate who, like several of his contemporaries, displayed an excess of rationalistic optimism in assuming that the scientific outlook would completely command the stage in mankind's future. If the scientific outlook were truly global, then all ideological conflicts based on ontological claims that were unverifiable or unfalsifiable would, quite simply, cease.

Comte's advocacy of positivism, for all its intensity, confined itself strictly to the task of describing the world. He did not, like Durkheim, see science as prescriptive as well as descriptive. In other words, he did not think that scientific knowledge could itself give us reasons for doing science. Reasons and motives for action were matters of ethics, not science, and were based on feelings, emotions, predilections. This distinction between the content of scientific activity and the reasons for performing such activity, plus the view that these reasons are affective, place Comte firmly in a tradition which can broadly be described as Humean. The tradition began with Hume in sharply distinguishing between facts and values, and in insisting that the latter cannot be derived from the former. For people in this tradition, scientific activity is undertaken to satisfy various emotional imperatives — not least the sheer desire or need for truth.

The emotivist theory of ethics, which remains a highly cogent one, led Comte to aver that one of the most important ethical and social tasks was to widen the range of unselfish and altruistic feeling. Since people acted, fundamentally, on the strength of their emotions, the route to social harmony and wellbeing was to increase the scope of those emotions which made for unity and mutuality.[3] This approach has obvious links with religion, particularly Christianity, at its rare best; but of course for Comte the perspective was humanistic; and all circumspect humanists will surely concur with it.

Comte's Durkheimian stress on the need for social harmony is bound up with his view of the fundamental oneness of the human race: a unity which was evident throughout history. This oneness consisted, firstly, in the primacy of emotion in the formation of motives for action; secondly, in man's constant need to act, to make his mark on the world around him; and thirdly, in his use of intelli-

---

[3] It is important to point out that Comte, like Durkheim but unlike Marx, did not think that violence was the solution to social and political problems. Solutions lay in changes of outlook and states of mind.

gence to act effectively, and so satisfy the emotions which underpinned his motives.

On the basis of this rather elementary picture of a permanent human nature, Comte builds a number of more complex and interesting arguments, in which he categorises different kinds of egoistic and altruistic feelings, plus different kinds of intellectual activity and willing. He claims that these various forms of emotion, thought and volition are permanent features of human behaviour, though they manifest themselves in various ways throughout history, according to the outlets and constraints of particular environments and milieux.[4]

The contention that there exists a fixed human essence has found parallels in subsequent thought, and is to be taken seriously. Reference has already been made to Pareto. Another names which could be mentioned are Santayana, Eliot, Freud and Jung. As long as we bear in mind the evolutionary perspective, and confine ourselves to humanity's present state of physical evolution and what we know of its capacities, there is indeed a case for arguing for recurring tendencies.

Finally, let us look at Comte's concept of a sociocracy. Like Durkheim, Comte recognised the individual's need to attach himself to something greater than himself, and saw that supernaturalistic outlooks could no longer meet this need. As a humanist, he argued that attachment could only legitimately be to something natural: namely, to the greatest human achievements in thought and action throughout the ages. Those individuals who had scaled the moral and cultural heights constituted a sociocracy, or, put another way, a social aristocracy — what we would now call a meritocracy. It was to this group that the rest of us should turn for guidance, sustenance, inspiration. Exceptional people transcended the human average, though not of course the human species, not humanity as a whole. Clearly, there is an overlap in Comte's thinking between the idea of

---

[4] Hence, for Comte, the study of history and social context remained very important. This could hardly have been otherwise for someone who was, after all, one of the founders of sociology. In fact, Comte made a leading contribution to the nineteenth century's ground-breaking work in historical and contextualist thinking.

Also, Comte's distinction between behavioural tendencies which were trans-historical, and particular manifestations of those tendencies which were located in specific historical moments, has affinities with Pareto's theory of residues and derivations.

sociocracy and that of an intellectual moral hierarchy of human beings.

Comte's notion of sociocracy makes him, in effect, an aristocratic humanist, someone with — to borrow Nietzschean terms — a vertical rather than a horizontal perspective. This perspective has a strong appeal for all humanists who insist on discriminating between exception and average, and who therefore reject the extreme form of democratic thinking which does not acknowledge this distinction. There is a very powerful argument indeed for maintaining a sense of meritocratic hierarchy among human beings,[5] and those who, in the present and the future, continue to espouse it will find lasting support in Comte.

---

[5] An argument nowhere better stated, incidentally, than in Ulysses's speech on status, reputation and order in Shakespeare's *Troilus and Cressida*.

Max Weber (1864–1920)

Amended text, reproduced by kind permission of 'Imprint Academic'.

Widely regarded as the greatest modern sociologist—certainly as the greatest German sociologist since Marx—Weber covered an encyclopaedic range of topics. Perhaps of chief interest to secularists are:

1) His exploration of religious culture, which was part of a project to enter sympathetically into the ethical outlooks and world-views of past societies, and so increase our imaginative understanding of the beliefs which sustained those societies. In this sensitive approach to the study of religion, he echoes Durkheim and Santayana.

2) His view that an absolute divide exists between facts and values, and that, therefore, the latter have to be chosen by an act of decision and will. There is no question of our factually *discovering* which values are right to choose. His keen sense of the difficulty of ethical choice prefigures Sartrean existentialism.

3) His conception of science as an on-going, indeed never-ending activity, in which positions are constantly being qualified, modified, amended or even abandoned. Hence, he differs radically from Comte, and anticipates twentieth century philosophers of science such as Popper.

4) In connection with his views on science, his awareness of the problems created by science's demystification of the natural world, its reduction of natural processes to ones which are useful to man but in themselves meaningless and without any sacred significance. Here, he foreshadows, among others, Heidegger, and harks back to the perplexities of the Romantic poets of the early nineteenth century.

5) His grasp of the enormous complexity of the social fabric: the inter-dependence of, and reciprocal inter-action between, society's many elements and components, with-

out any one single component's being primary or ultimate as a causal factor. This pluralistic outlook is as needed today as it ever was, given the persistence of monolithic and reductionist versions of social causation.

6) His concern for the integrity of the individual in the face of the increasing bureaucratisation of modern life: the widening threat to personhood of the growth of vast, anonymous organisations, both economic and political. This concern again links with existentialism. Also, Weber's interest in the individual led him to insist that particular people play a crucial role in history, over and above that played by general tendencies of a social and economic character.

Weber's studies of religious culture were wide-ranging. He examined Judaism, Hinduism and Buddhism, Taoism and Confucianism. However, his best known work in this field is on Christianity, or rather on one aspect of Christianity: *The Protestant Ethic and the Spirit of Capitalism*. In fact, this book does not even deal with the whole of Protestantism, but focuses on Calvinism. Weber argued that the growth of capitalism in North Western Europe was partly due to Calvinist ideas about a connection between the notion of personal salvation and a certain kind of economic activity. Without exploring the thesis in detail, it is sufficient to say that his reasoning goes against orthodox Marxism by contending that ideas and states of consciousness—which are not themselves merely reflexes of socio-economic conditions—can contribute to the shaping of an economic system and way of life. Marxist orthodoxy, by contrast, argues that economic systems are always the ultimate—most decisive—causes of ideas and states of consciousness: so, never ultimately effects of the latter. According to Weber, however, the economic system of capitalism was partly an effect of a set of ideas, that of Calvinism.

Weber's thesis reflects his intense interest in past societies, their ways of thinking and their value-systems. Also, it evidences his enormous historical erudition: he has been described as the last of the major sociologists with an encyclopaedic knowledge of world history. This panoramic sense of the human past in all its cultural and psychological variety is vital to humanism and secularism.[1] In

---

[1] As is attested by, for example, the writings of one of British secularism's greatest figures, Harold Blackham. See in particular Blackham's *The Future of Our Past*.

addition, his argument powerfully exemplifies his general view that social formations never have a primary or ultimate determinant: Calvinism was seen by Weber as, to repeat, only one cause of capitalism: there were other causes as well.

While deeply interested in religious culture, Weber nevertheless stood back from all religions and saw moral values, not as objects of divinely-instigated revelation, but as products of human choice and decision. They were chosen; not deduced from facts, and therefore not from science. Weber is, then, part of the post-Humean tradition of moral subjectivism and non-cognitivism. In this respect, he is like Comte but unlike Durkheim. However, more so than Comte, he perceived the problems in having to decide on values with no scientific, let alone theological or metaphysical, guidance for support. His work conveys the anxiety and drama of choice in ways which anticipate Sartre (as said) and the whole field of atheistic existentialism.

His perception of difficulty was heightened by an awareness of the problem of conflict between different value-systems, as held by different groups, societies, cultures; and of the impossibility of resolving the conflict by appealing to purely objective criteria. For Weber, as for every secularist, no such criteria exist: all is relative, all contingent. To speak figuratively, the gods of Olympus are in conflict, and even Zeus cannot be objective arbiter. Weber's meditations on this topic parallel those of Isaiah Berlin.[2]

Though mankind could not look to science for moral guidance, still science held for Weber a central place in the human adventure, as the region of ontological questing. It was a region, however, without boundaries, and humanity would have to accept this. The labour and toil would be endless, with no completion or final stage reachable. In particular, no certain knowledge of the future was possible. The pertinence of this view to contemporary perspectives in science, chiefly physics, is clear. Also, it is interesting to note that Weber's view was that causal laws, as formulated thus far, were only probably applicable to future experience. This position accords with the non-dogmatic character of law-concepts in modern physics.

Even if the scientific project was, by its nature, uncompletable, still science had done enough thus far to banish forever, for its adherents, the mythopoeic, magical, enchanted and sacred view of the natural world held by almost all pre-scientific cultures. Weber had unflinching insight into the psychological difficulties created by the sense of

---

[2] Further, the theme of moral conflict, it hardly needs to be said, is perennially central to great literature, especially drama.

Max Weber (1864–1920)

nature as a totally neutral, impersonal dimension, one that could be controlled and exploited, but one that was no longer a friend, equivalent or even superior[3] to man. (The transition from the latter metaphysical view to the former is in fact what Comte refers to when he speaks of the movement to positivism and a strictly scientific outlook.) For Weber, man could no longer project himself outward onto the natural world, and so identify with it. From this inability came a sense of cosmic homelessness. As said, these difficulties were explored by the Romantic poets before Weber, and by Heidegger and others[4] after him. The difficulties of course remain.

The problem of inability to identify with the natural world was, for Weber, matched by one of equal magnitude: the danger of the individual's being submerged in the man-made world of huge, impersonal and bureaucratic organisations. Weber saw large-scale organisation and bureaucratisation as in fact the distinctive feature of modern life (whereas Durkheim, conversely, had seen that distinctive feature as differentiation between individuals). In regarding mass-organisation as the fundamental tendency, Weber feared that the individual sphere would be irremediably damaged and stunted. In this respect, he shows himself to be a classical liberal.(His writings on this subject remind one strongly of, for example, those of Russell.) They also strike, again, an existentialist note: the protest against society's 'pigeon-holing' of the individual, a protest which is so prominent a feature of existentialist thought, secular and religious.

Weber's anxieties grew out of his experience of capitalist society, and it is clear that this form of society, in its industrial, commercial and other structures, has indeed moved in a direction to justify those anxieties. At the same time, Weber thought that a socialist kind of society, were it to emerge, would also subordinate the individual to large, anonymous institutions: again, because this tendency was endemic to modern times. Indeed, Weber feared that, under socialism, the subordination of the individual would be even more severe. On this point, it is worth noting that his death in 1920 came only three years after the establishment of the U.S.S.R. While the latter's regime would not now be generally regarded as having been socialist, 'socialist' is what it called itself; and, had Weber lived, he would

---

[3] The notion of nature as a superior is found, for example, in Wordsworth's view that receptivity to nature can be a source of moral education for man.
[4] These others include, again, existentialists, with whom Heidegger can be broadly associated.

have undoubtedly found confirmation of his worst fears in the spectacle of Stalinism in the Soviet Union. A similar point could be made about Chinese 'socialism' after 1949.

One aspect of Weber's misgivings regarding the individual and mass-institutions was that, the more tightly organised and bureaucratised society became, the more fixed and rigidly demarcated became the individual's occupational role. This is actually a long-standing issue in sociology, bound up with the fact of extreme division of labour in the modern world, and one which deeply exercised Marx in the nineteenth century. However, whereas Marx saw the problem only in the context of capitalism, Weber, as we have noted, viewed matters in the context of modernity as a whole.

The restriction of the role of the individual, in occupational thought and action, was all the more problematic in that he could not look beyond the man-made sphere to the natural world as an area with which to identify. Nevertheless, there was, in Weber's eyes, a form of liberation—at least mental liberation—available, and this was political: giving support to outstanding people who were charismatic political leaders and who transcended the constrained circumstances under which most people lived. This giving of support was for Weber an inviolable right for the individual to exercise; it constituted a freedom otherwise denied by his conditions of daily life.

Weber's interest in charismatic leaders as figures who offer society something extraordinary, as a welcome contrast to the commonplace, banal and bureaucratic, is connected with his view of the importance in history of outstanding individuals. While recognising the significance of large-scale impersonal forces and 'massive facts'—social, economic, cultural—he nevertheless regarded these factors as always leaving a margin for individuals to take decisive action and so tip the scales. This area of individual input, combined with the play of arbitrary circumstances and accidents, meant that there were no laws of history which predetermined the course of events: no laws, therefore, the knowledge of which would bestow clairvoyance. In this, Weber again strongly reminds us of Russell, and also of the emphatic anti-historicism of Popper. Further, we recall that Weber's concept of physical law was non-dogmatic. Overall, his opposition to the notion of historical determinism is one which most contemporary secularists share.

Returning now to Weber's point about what exceptional leaders can offer modern society: while his argument clearly has merit, it is actually the only one in the group we have been examining which contains highly questionable implications. Its merit lies in its recognition of the value of the extraordinary, and in the distinction it draws between the exceptional and the mediocre. These evaluations are ones which modern society should certainly retain. On the other hand, there is obvious danger in a situation where enormous numbers of people look to certain individuals and their sphere of leadership activity, solely as an uplifting contrast to their own ways of life. If their own life-styles are hemmed in by mass-organisation and bureaucracy, then there is a strong possibility that they will transfer their enthusiasm and commitment almost entirely to those individuals who are not thus restricted, and so engage, in effect, in hero-worship. It scarcely needs saying that hero-worship is insidious for the worshippers and the worshipped. Had Weber lived longer, he would have witnessed in his own country what is probably the most monstrous example of this phenomenon in recorded history.

It is true that he regarded bureaucratisation as endemic, and so we can see why he viewed charismatic leadership as the only meaningful contrast to it. Also, we can sympathise with the frustrations felt by all those who work in highly bureaucratic organisations. But the question we must ask is: Can bureaucracy and impersonality be radically reduced, given sustained effort? Many people will reply in the positive, and will indeed point to a number of developments in contemporary society where such reduction is actually being achieved. For example, there has been the growth of small-scale communitarian and NGO organisations which, because of their smallness and inner dynamic, avoid bureaucratisation. The larger the area for individual fulfilment, self-fashioning and creative co-operation with others, the smaller will be the need to look beyond one's own sphere of activity and experience to one that is remote, probably idealised, and seen virtually as a substitute for one's own context. Society should be of such a kind that no-one is led to live at a heightened level by proxy; that level should be directly available to all. This position is surely at the heart of the liberalism with which Weber, at his best, can be identified.

To Weber's failure to perceive a wider range of ways in which modern society can develop must be added what many people would regard as another shortcoming: his intense nationalism. This nationalism may seem odd in the light of the fact that almost all the Weberian issues we have been examining are universally relevant to modern man, regardless of country. Yet Weber was a nationalist, despite his liberalism and generally complex ways of thinking. This was displayed in his contention that Germany should take its place among the world powers, since power was an expression of human greatness. Hindsight enables us to be critical of nationalism in all its forms, when viewed as a basis for acquiring power over other nations or for adopting a hostile stance toward them. That kind of perspective was a factor in the general European colonialism of the nineteenth century, and contributed to the outbreak of two world wars in the twentieth. It of course remains a problem in the twenty-first century.

However, these negative criticisms of Weber apart, let us briefly and finally return to those elements in his work which remain valid and contemporary. His imaginative and empathetic approach to the past, especially the religious past; his view of science as open-ended, and as having irreversibly transformed our cosmic outlook; his perspective on ethics as a field of difficult decision-making; his richly complex sense of what constitutes society; and his concern with the individual under threat from bureaucracy and impersonality: all these themes mark him as a key figure for secularists and for all panoramically-minded people of today.

The Poetry of Matthew Arnold

This essay will briefly re-affirm a well established view about Arnold's poetry: that it is urgently modern in many of its themes and concerns. Such re-affirmation is continually necessary, given the on-going relevance of those themes and concerns to modern experience, at least to that in Western society.

Let's begin by asking: How can that experience be characterised, in relation to people of genuinely open and searching minds? Its chief feature has been the questioning and even rejection of a number of beliefs and assumptions which had been prevalent in the West until, broadly speaking, the nineteenth century—or, more precisely, till the second half of that century. These beliefs and assumptions were mainly bound up with traditional Christianity and, by the period in question, were coming under increasingly heavy fire from empirical science: an assault which has of course continued. Religious postulates such as those about the existence of deity, the origin of the universe and of mankind, and the fundamental components of reality, were being dealt severe blows, and have suffered even severer ones since. One result of this erosion of positions which had been entrenched for centuries was, and remains, a sense of ontological uncertainty. The question of the ultimate nature of reality loomed, as it still does, as one with no clear or final answer.

This issue is among many which Arnold's poetry explores. His thematic range is very wide, and the general modernity of his subject-matter comes home to the reader in the most striking manner: partly through diction which often possesses a definitive authority in articulating the point to be conveyed. Arguably, his work, produced mostly in the 1850s and 60s, carries more relevance to our time than that of his fellow mid-Victorians, Tennyson and Browning, and in this respect equals that of Hardy, the leading English poet of the late-Victorian and immediate post-Victorian period.

In addition to ontological doubt, the other concerns in Arnold's work which are equally modern in impact are ethical, but closely related to the ontological. These include: the difficulty of in-depth communication between individuals; the problem of maintaining integrity, and indeed understanding, of self in the face of society's complex pressures and demands; the accompanying difficulty of giving one's life sustained meaning and direction, one actuated by passionate commitment; and the risks arising from breaking with convention and following one's own independent path.

On the ontological issue, perhaps the best place to start is with one of Arnold's most famous poems, 'Dover Beach'. Here he refers, briefly but unforgettably, to the loss of religious faith which was such a marked feature of his time and of his own life. He speaks of hearing the "melancholy, long, withdrawing roar" of "The Sea of Faith", and goes on to present a world-view shorn of the false assurances which religious belief once provided. In this perspective, the non-human physical sphere is gaunt and harsh; the Sea of Faith retreats "down the vast edges drear/And naked shingles of the world"; and reality as a whole contains "neither joy, nor love, nor light,/Nor certitude, nor peace, nor help for pain."

At the same time, this outlook carries ethical implications. Precisely because human beings are situated in a godless reality, Arnold urges fidelity in personal relationships: "Ah, love, let us be true/To one another." Such sense of the supreme value of personal relationships is one which many people have shared in the largely post-religious context of modern times.

Whereas 'Dover Beach' includes strong moral affirmation, despite the ontological vision conveyed, this is not the case in 'Stanzas from the Grande Chartreuse'. Here, loss of faith is not compensated for by ethical assertion. Arnold speaks of himself as having shed his faith but as having found no vigorous life-stance with which to replace that loss. He is "Wandering between two worlds, one dead,/The other powerless to be born ... on earth I wait forlorn."

He adds that his own state of moral and psychological limbo is widespread—is, indeed, characteristic of the time: "the best are silent now ... The kings of modern thought are dumb." This situation has persisted in Western culture: the bafflement of high intelligence remains a central experience, especially in the light of the formidable increase in scientific data which the twentieth century has witnessed, and the problem of mentally encompassing that data. Arnold's words have since been echoed by Yeats: "the best lack all conviction" (in 'The Second Coming'.)

The moral commitment which would be an escape from limbo cannot, for Arnold, be found through attachment, Wordsworth-style, to the natural world. If the super-natural does not exist as a goal for ethical involvement, then the natural sphere, though indubitably existent, does not provide that goal either. This point, made briefly in 'Dover Beach', is explored in some detail in the ironically titled 'In Harmony with Nature'. Arnold avers that nature is too harsh a medium for man to identify with: "Nature is cruel, man is sick of blood". (Compare, incidentally, Tennyson's "Nature red in tooth and claw".) He argues that man is unique, the most complex part of the natural world, and that his distinctively human needs and aspirations cannot be met by anything external to the human species: "man hath all which Nature hath, but more,/And in that *more* lie all his hopes of good ... Man must begin ... Where Nature ends." Hence humanity, though situated within nature, is species-isolated in the sense that it can find no equivalent or even near-equivalent to itself in the natural world. This view of mankind has, since Arnold's day, gained continual reinforcement from neo-Darwinism and is now a main plank of evolutionary humanism.

One of Arnold's most detailed explorations of ontology comes in his long poem 'Empedocles on Etna'. He examines the idea of possessing total knowledge of reality, seeing such knowledge as intuitive rather than derived from systematic reasoning, but also as debarred from us while we remain "prisoners of our consciousness" (l. 352). As part of this argument, he presents the notion of an "All" which mind and thought only allow us to see "through their forms, and modes, and stifling veils" (l. 354). Here Arnold is, whether consciously or not, presenting a philosophical doctrine: that of epistemological idealism, according to which the mind's ways ("forms, modes, and stifling veils") of apprehending the external world deliver to consciousness only a subjective version of that externality: a version presenting a divided and fragmented picture of a reality which is—in itself, objectively—unified, undivided, undifferentiated. This doctrine, in Arnold's own time, was most closely associated with Schopenhauer, who was extensively influenced by Kant. It remains an important line of thinking in modern philosophy, which is much concerned with the essentially Kantian issue of the problems surrounding human effort to gain objective knowledge of the world. At the same time, in the domain of physics, increasing strength has been lent to the postulate that reality is actually unitary—that every entity in the universe consists of one substance: energy.

As to expressing the perennial experience of feeling unable to accede to a total comprehension of reality—and especially the frustration and bewilderment felt by the youthfully eager and questing mind—few poetic images can surpass Arnold's metaphor of the mirror:

> Hither and thither spins
> The wind-borne, mirroring soul,
> A thousand glimpses wins,
> And never sees the whole (ll. 82–5).

Arnold's grappling with ontological issues minus the support of religious doctrine produces a number of statements on the difficulty of attaining certain truth of any kind. For example, in 'Thyrsis', he declares that

> long the way [to truth] appears, which seemed so short
> To the less practiced eye of sanguine youth;
> And high the mountain-tops, in cloudy air,
> The mountain-tops where is the throne of Truth,
> Tops in life's morning sun so bright and bare!

This can be linked with his sense of the unforeseeable dangers that the isolated, truth-seeking mind may fall into, as conveyed in 'Empedocles on Etna' by the extended phrase: "some fantastic maze/Forged by the imperious lonely thinking-power" (ll. 375–6).

The above words put us in mind of Hardy. In connection with the latter's work, the critic Irving Howe speaks of

> a cluster of assumptions central to modernist literature: that in our time men wishing to be more than dumb clods must live in permanent doubt and intellectual crisis; that for such men, to whom traditional beliefs are no longer available, life has become inherently problematic; that in the course of their years they must face even more than the usual allotment of loneliness and anguish.[a]

If this characterisation of modern literature is accurate, then Arnold's work is as modernist as Hardy's. In the ways indicated by Howe, both men anticipate a large area of twentieth century writing, especially that of existentialists such as Sartre.

Let's move on now to Arnold's primarily ethical issues. Firstly, the difficulty of in-depth communication between individuals: one of the most poignant delineations of this problem comes in 'From Switzerland', where Arnold describes the mutual estrangement between himself and his former mistress, Marguerite. Both people are depicted as incapable of any fully-fledged attachment to another person because of their recurrent tendency to self-absorption and consequent need for solitude.

In tension with this tendency, there is a longing for full and permanent union with another—"a longing like despair", as Arnold puts it, but one seen as unlikely of fulfilment because

> in the sea of life enisled,
> With echoing straits between us thrown,
> Dotting the shoreless watery wild,
> We mortal millions live alone.

Isolation, then, is regarded as a fundamental feature of the human condition. Also, we should note in Arnold's choice of imagery a physical grimness which recalls that of 'Dover Beach'. Here, ontological considerations re-enter: Arnold appears to be linking loneliness with the absence of any religious ontology, acceptance of which could offer a release from solitude.

The modernity of this focus on isolation is clear. In relation to its obvious link with the Howe quotation above, examples of the theme of loneliness in modern literature abound, particularly in drama. For instance, one immediately thinks of the words of Tennessee Williams when he describes

> this always thwarted effort to break through walls to each other. As a character in a play once said, 'We're all of us sentenced to solitary confinement inside our own skins'.[b]

Among dramatists, one also thinks of Samuel Beckett, with his view that loneliness is man's existential fate. Among other other authors in general, examples include Conrad, Graham Greene, Somerset Maugham and, again, Sartre.

Now to the problem of maintaining integrity, and even understanding, of self in the face of social pressures and demands. In this regard, two of Arnold's most important poems are 'The Scholar-Gipsy' and 'The Buried Life'. In the former, Arnold sees as a moral exemplar the young scholar who gave up all conventional ambitions in order to pursue his internal spiritual development. In showing the courage to jettison all thought of security and social status, he released himself from the spiritually destructive pressures which social conformity entails.

This said, it has to be acknowledged that the specific image of the scholar-gipsy now strikes many people as quaint and out-dated, as linked with the 'bohemian' attitudes which permeated various kinds of social rebelliousness in the nineteenth and early twentieth centuries. More recent notions of social rebellion have been more complex, less picturesque or romantic in conception. The charge of quaintness is a fair one.

Nevertheless, it is arguable that the poem still retains a great deal of force, chiefly because of its concentration on two general points: the importance of the individual's being focussed and resolute in intellectual and spiritual aspirations, and the undeniably deleterious effects which social pressure can have on those aspirations. No reader genuinely concerned with self-development will fail to be inspired by Arnold's description of the scholar as having "*one* aim, *one* business, *one* desire", and as possessing powers "Fresh, undiverted to the world without,/Firm to their mark, not spent on other things." Also, no reader with extended experience of the modern workaday world will fail to understand Arnold when he asks,

> For what wears out the life of mortal men?
> 'Tis that repeated shocks, again, again,
> Exhaust the energy of strongest souls.

Instant recognition will again register with Arnold's characterisation of

> this strange disease of modern life,
> With its sick hurry, its divided aims,
> Its heads o'ertax'd, its palsied hearts ...

Another powerful aspect of the poem, again with clear contemporary relevance, is the depiction of those people who are discontented with subjection to conventional demands but, unlike the scholar-gipsy, lack the resolve to break from them. These are ones

> Who fluctuate idly without term or scope,
> Of whom each strives, nor knows for what he strives,
> And each half lives a hundred different lives ...
> Who never deeply felt, nor clearly willed,
> Whose insight never has borne fruit in deeds ...
> Who hesitate and falter life away ...

Arnold's trenchant diction combines critical force with deep comprehension.

Overall, the poem achieves the difficult feat of effectively empathising both with behaviour which is praiseworthy and with that which is not. Success of this kind highlights the modernity of the poem: it is about the almost overpowering complexity of modern social reality, in which non-fulfilment, just as much as fulfilment, calls for detailed commentary.

In "The Buried Life", there is a certain relaxation of the polarity, found in 'The Scholar-Gipsy,' between self-fulfilment and non-fulfilment that are total. Here, encounter with one's essential self is shown as partially realisable amid the distractions of the everyday world, and sometimes in the context of a genuinely intimate relationship with another. In such moments,

> A man becomes aware of his life's flow,
> And hears its winding murmur
> ... And then he thinks he knows
> The hills where his life rose,
> And the sea where it goes.

But, Arnold adds, these are only moments, and for most people the painful reality is that

> hardly have we, for one little hour,
> Been on our own line, have we been ourselves —
> Hardly had skill to utter one of all
> The nameless feelings that course through our breast,
> But they course on forever unexpress'd.

Then, says Arnold, we are back in thrall to the social constraints and diversions which have previously blocked true engagement with self. Manifestly, such experience finds its counterpart in the contemporary world — where, indeed, the external pressures and distractions are even more numerous than they were in Arnold's day.

Sustained self-encounter, very difficult though it is to achieve, is for Arnold indispensable for inner peace. Despite all the immense obstacles he knows to stand in its way, he urges the reader, in 'Self-Dependence', to "Resolve to be thyself; and know that he,/Who finds himself, loses his misery!" Similarly, in 'Empedocles on Etna', he declares that, in being one with our "deep-buried selves", "we are one with the whole world" (ll.371–2).

Pursuit of self-encounter and self-development is, in the language of twentieth century existentialism, pursuit of authentic existence. This, for Arnold, means taking risks with one's life. Arnold's examination of risk is shown in 'The Scholar-Gipsy', as we have seen, but it is evident in other poems too: notably, 'A Summer's Night' and 'Rugby Chapel'.

In the former, Arnold begins by re-iterating his critique of social conformity, which includes economic dependence, with words which, as much as any quoted so far, carry definitive authority. They describe the working lives of most people in Arnold's time, and perhaps most — certainly many — in modern times as well:

> For most men in a brazen prison live,
> Where, in the sun's hot eye,
> With heads bent o'er their toil, they languidly

> Their lives to some unmeaning taskwork give,
> Dreaming of nought beyond their prison-wall.

Arnold then describes how a few rebel against their constrictions, and attempt a new kind of life, following their aspirations without regard of social and economic consequences. Deploying dramatic nautical imagery, he shows how such people may, despite courage and tenacity, fail completely in their project, in the process losing whatever social and economic security they previously possessed. They may even be driven to suicide. So, the emancipated individual, sailing

> the wide ocean of life anew ... braves
> The freshening wind and blackening waves.
> And then the tempest strikes him ... And sterner comes the roar
> Of sea and wind, and through the deepening gloom
> Fainter and fainter wreck and helmsman loom,
> And he too disappears, and comes no more.

It is true that, in modern Western society, the dangers involved in radical life-experimentation are less severe than in Arnold's time, when there was virtually no state provision for those bereft of social and economic security; but such dangers still exist, and Arnold's point will not be lost on the modern reader.

In "Rugby Chapel", the situation is not as dire—it is about not failure and extinction but endurance and survival. However, survival is depicted as solitary and unshared. The enterprise described is the quest for profound insight, undertaken by a minority of human beings who are separated from the majority by "a thirst,/ Ardent, unquenchable" for "something to snatch/From dull oblivion". But the journey to enlightenment is long and hard, through—figuratively speaking—dizzying and storm-lashed terrain. The minority who originally set off all perish, except for one; he alone reaches the destination, "Stripp'd, without friends..."

Arnold's poetic material serves as a powerful allegory of intellectual isolation, as experienced by the mind which, through extraordinary effort and tenacity, has outspaced its contemporaries. To extend a point previously made, such experience is as much of the present as of the past. When, for example, the man widely regarded as the greatest twentieth century philosopher, Russell, writes that "I have felt since early youth the pain of solitude",[c] we see a preeminent modern instance of the mental loneliness, entailed by in-depth thinking, which Arnold knew in a nineteenth century context.

Clearly, in his ontological and ethical explorations, Arnold is the poet of the perennially problematic. It is of course true that all major poets are problematists of this kind, in varying degree; it need only be specified that Arnold was one to the highest degree.

More generally, it is the urgency and weightiness of his ideas which are perhaps the main factors placing him in the front rank. While he cannot compare with Tennyson in range of technical mastery and musicality, nor with Browning in creation of character, he surpasses both, as previously said, in intellectual modernity. Intense and immediate engagement with broad themes, though ones always related to personal experience, is his hallmark.

One last theme can be briefly looked at: a political one. In "Continued", he expresses scepticism about revolutionary politics and the prospect of achieving universal harmony among mankind. He implies that humanity is not the possessor of unlimited capacities but is subject to inherent limitations which result from causal processes; and therefore cannot achieve all the things which extreme political idealism hopes for:

> this earth
> Whereon we dream,
> Is on all sides o'ershadow'd by the high
> Uno'erleap'd Mountains of Necessity,
> Sparing us narrower margin than we deem.

Also, selfishness will not easily or quickly be overcome; it will not suddenly cease "at a human nod".

In these cautious and cautionary observations, Arnold shows a penetrating insight into political affairs both past and present. Political experience in both the nineteenth and twentieth centuries has repeatedly highlighted the problems to which Arnold refers, and the likelihood is that such problems will persist.

Arnold's panoramic grasp of the fundamental difficulties and complexities of being human is quintessentially conveyed in the closing lines of his poem "Shakespeare". Shakespeare's triumph, he avers, was to voice "All pains the immortal spirit must endure,/All weakness that impairs, all griefs that bow".

End Notes

[a]   Howe, *Thomas Hardy* (London: Weidenfeld and Nicholson, 1968), pp. 134–5.
[b]   In *Cat on a Hot Tin Roof and Other Plays* (Penguin Books, 1976), p. 7.
[c]   In *Autobiography* (London: Unwin Paperbacks, 1967), p. 261.

The Challenge of Major Literature

Matthew Arnold's famous definition of poetry as "a criticism of life" applies in fact to all literary genres. One reason for this is that the word "criticism" partly means description and depiction, and all genres, where they have excelled, have done so partly by their descriptive breadth and depth: by the extent of their account of human experience, thought, feeling, inter-action.

Because of its depictive range and accuracy, major writing has always been a challenge to the social mainstream—as, indeed, has every instance of such accuracy: eminent work in the sciences and in philosophy also springs to mind. Descriptive magnitude and precision are invariably a challenge because they attack the superficialities, oversimplifications, complacencies and evasions which unfortunately constitute, at all times, a considerable part of the general social mentality.

Nonetheless, the challenge is perhaps more conspicuous today, at least in contemporary Western society, than in the past. The in-depth depiction of experience is at odds with the mainstream, 'official' view of what significant experience consists of. What is this view? Basically, it is that significant experience is chiefly a matter of achieving occupational and economic success and (though nowadays less emphasised) domestic stability and harmony. This position does, it is true, recognise the reality of situations which do not fall under these headings, but sees them as merely perverse forms of experience situated at the shadow-edge of society: as unnecessary complexities which the social collective can well do without, and which should, if possible, be resolved as quickly as possible.

The notion of resolving problems, undoing complications and overcoming difficulties is pivotal to the 'official' outlook, precisely because its chief values are social harmony and efficiency, and its principal goal the smooth-running of the social mechanism. This attitude relates most obviously to the economic system—and would do so, it should be noted, to any such system, whether the capitalist one which is currently dominant, or a socialist one. But, beyond this, it relates to *all* aspects of social inter-action where the objective is to maximise integration and smooth operation.

This outlook is essentially homocentric, though not humanistic in the most capacious sense of that term: a point to which we will return. Also, the outlook may well be one which did not exist in Western society, or at least did not exist to anything like the same extent, before the nineteenth century. Whatever the precise historical truth in this regard, the fact is that such an 'official' perspective does now obtain, and has done so for well over a century. Its emergence was probably due, in the main, to the unprecedented degree of social and economic organisation reached in the West by the late nineteenth century. Its marked intensification, in the second half of the twentieth century, has chiefly resulted from the radical widening of educational and economic opportunity in this period.

It can be reasonably assumed that there was less emphasis on thorough-going social integration in earlier, less tightly co-ordinated forms of society in the West. There was simply more psychological room, even within the framework of the daily round, for thinking beyond the confines of integrative and strictly functional activity. Also, it is arguable that there was more of a response to literature which accurately described and explored the kinds of problems, complications and predicaments that modern advocates of social efficiency regard as having little or no intrinsic importance. The response was wider because minds less under pressure to conform to a standardised social outlook were more alive to the dark lacunae found between the everyday norms of experience.

The literary form producing the widest response was drama, since an appreciation of it did not depend on literacy; and ,of dramatic forms, tragedy was the one which focussed the most intensely on the dark areas of experience. Its subject was, and remains, the intractable and insoluble predicament; hence, on-going mental suffering. Of major significance is the fact that, thus far in Western literature, the three greatest efflorescences of tragic drama[1] belong to the distant past. The last of the three was in the seventeenth century in France, its leading figures being Racine and Corneille. The one prior to that was the sixteenth and early seventeenth centuries in England, with Shakespeare and Marlowe as its most prominent authors. The first

---

[1] The 'greatest' but not, of course, the only. The early nineteenth century saw significant production of tragic drama in Germany, with Goethe the main figure, and in the late nineteenth century there was Ibsen. This output was major, but lacks the apex-power of that in the three periods specified above.

lies nearly two thousand years before Shakespeare: the fifth and fourth centuries BC, in Greece, its luminaries being Aeschylus, Sophocles and Euripides. The societies in which these flowerings occurred were of course different from each other (though England in the sixteenth and France in the seventeenth centuries were less dissimilar than either was, in a number of respects, to ancient Greece). But what they all had in common was a very exploratory approach to experience, one ensuring freedom from the modern dogma that the most meaningful kinds of experience are those which enhance the smooth running of social and economic processes.

This exploratory approach is perhaps best exemplified in classic passages from Shakespeare's *Hamlet* and Sophocles's *Oedipus at Colonus*, both of which detail the perennial ills of existence, including the encounters with adversity, antipathy and inconstancy. The passages, though composed almost two millennia apart, are strikingly similar not only in content but also phrasing. They are exploratory in that they break completely from complacency, evasion and illusion, and delve to the harsh truths which form a large part of the bedrock of our lives. In doing so, they reach, like all great tragedy, the profoundest levels of expressive power and poignancy. (In this connection, it is worth remembering that almost all the finest tragedies were written, wholly or mainly, in verse — were poetic drama.)

These observations on tragic drama do not overlook the facts that religion was a prominent feature of the cultures in these societies, and that religious belief is an integrative force. But commitment to religion, assuming it actually existed among the majority in these societies, was commitment to a transcendental doctrine of some kind, and so was unlike the modern adherence to social and economic efficiency. Another consideration is that, in the case of France in the seventeenth century and, to a lesser extent, England in the sixteenth, an important religious influence was Christian Catholicism: which, at this time, emphasised human frailty and proneness to tragic error, and was therefore very sceptical about notions of social efficiency and pervasive harmony.

By contrast, the modern doctrine of efficiency has, to repeat, no transcendental dimension, or at least none that is indispensable to it. Its doctrine is, to all intents and purposes, immanent, and — as said earlier — homocentric, not theocentric. More importantly, it is function-based, and therefore cannot have the dauntlessly searching approach to experience to be found in a religious-transcendental view and — arguably even more so — in a highly complex humanistic view. Radically probing curiosity, shedding extensive light on human weakness and misadventure, always moves beyond doctrines of functional efficiency.

Returning to the tragic drama of the past: its focus on the intractable and incurable predicament was, as said, probably less of a challenge to the societies in which it was performed because those societies were less functionalist in outlook. Again, the reverse is true in modern society, because of its highly functionalist perspective.

The latter is the case even though modern tragedy differs radically in some ways from the traditional kind. In the plays of Sophocles, Shakespeare and Racine, the tragic protagonist, whose virtues are undermined by a fatal weakness entailing pain and failure, is a person of high social standing. This social position reflects the aristocratic focus of the cultures in which these plays were written. But in modern tragedy, the traditional social pattern is broken, with a focus on different kinds of people in different social locations. See the protagonists in plays by, for example, Eugene O'Neill, Tennessee Williams, Jean Anouilh and Samuel Beckett. Such variety clearly reflects the more democratic character of present society.

Yet despite these important differences, modern tragic drama remains allied to its predecessors in delineating the insoluble situation. Thus it continues the millennia-spanning practice of foregrounding the fact of deep-seated suffering as a fundamental feature of the human condition. However, once again, it does so in a social climate much less favourable to the reception of that fact than were previous ones.

At the same time, the unfavourableness of the contemporary context confers, arguably, greater importance on modern tragedy than on its predecessors. On its shoulders rests a larger responsibility for sensitising society to the full spectrum of experience: for, that is, expanding consciousness. From any serious moral perspective, such expansion is surely self-justifying, whatever its consequences.

Further, in discharging this responsibility, modern tragedy links up with that significant number of people who emphatically reject the view that social efficiency is all-important. Many of these people lack the articulateness of the literary artist, and so need the latter to voice the feelings they share with him but cannot effectively express. To these people especially, then, the tragic dramatist performs a vital service.

Tragic drama is a lesson in the realism which constantly reminds that utopian notions of experience are invalid: notions which are at least implicit in the 'official' view under discussion. In this very broad sense, tragedy is educational, widening awareness in a way that is absolutely necessary for retaining a sense of the permanent possibility of pitfall, of plunge into the irremediable.

But of course the same general lesson on non-utopianism can come from other literary sources as well, when they are adequately descriptive: from fiction, poetry and — not to be under-rated — comic drama. Just as much as tragedy, these have provided the outlet for conveying a vision of things which, by virtue of its range and complexity, outspaces the 'official' view. Irony, humour, grasp of the ambiguous, the ambivalent and the contradictory: these too are indicators of experiences unvalued by the dogma of functionalism — and arrows fired at that dogma, hitting their target.

Overall, major literature of all kinds does what all major disciplines do: it induces an attitude to the world which is, in sizeable measure, contemplative. Thus it obviously clashes with out-and-out functionalism. Whether we use Arnold's words "a criticism of life" or James Joyce's phrase "luminous stasis", we are talking about the valuing of perceptions and insights for what they are in themselves, not for what practical activities they might lead on to.

E.M. Forster said that organised society, in whatever form, could only provide space for expression of part of the human spirit, and that the other part could only be expressed in art. If this is accepted as true, then clearly no form of social involvement can ever fully replace the role played by artistic activity. We should immediately add that this is not something to regret. It is good that such a divide should exist, since each side of it can provide different kinds of satisfaction and fulfilment: perhaps kinds which supplement each other. But the social side will only provide satisfaction if it is flexible and complex in outlook — and this the doctrine of social efficiency is obviously *not*. Hence mainstream society needs to relax its rigidity, slow its pace, show an appreciation of the vast intricacy of things. Only then will its participants be able to breathe more easily, and feel less anxious about preserving their personal identity and deepest insights, while in its midst. Only then will the tension between the values of the private and the public be reduced. Finally, only then will major literature, and the whole field of artistic expression, be less of a challenge to the social mainstream than they inevitably and rightfully are at present.

Modern Literature: Some Challenges

In the previous essay, it was argued that major literature in general challenges the social mainstream by depicting areas of experience which are too complex to be compatible with narrow doctrines of social efficiency. The present essay is premised on the same argument, but focuses specifically on modern literature, and explores some of the distinctive kinds of challenge it presents to perfunctory social attitudes. By 'modern literature' is meant Western literature from, roughly, the mid nineteenth century.

Let's begin with a previously cited quotation from the critic Irving Howe on Thomas Hardy, a writer who became prominent in the later part of the nineteenth century. Commenting on Hardy's novel *Jude the Obscure* (1895), Howe says that the book contains

> a cluster of assumptions central to modernist literature: that in our time men wishing to be more than dumb clods must live in permanent doubt and intellectual crisis; that for such men, to whom traditional beliefs are no longer available, life has become inherently problematic; that in the course of their days they must face even more than the usual allotment of loneliness and anguish ... that courage, if it is to be found at all, consists in a readiness to accept pain while refusing the comforts of certainty.[a]

Perhaps the three key points in this passage are: the decline of "traditional beliefs," which can be safely assumed to be the demise mainly of religious faith, chiefly of Christianity; the taxing implications of that demise—intellectually, emotionally, even socially; and the consequent need for a stoical attitude. These are all points about having to shoulder burdens; and Howe is in essence saying that modernist literature is largely an exploration of intellectual predicament.

For more material on this predicament, let's now go to Hardy himself. In his novel *The Return of the Native* (1878), he describes as follows the countenance of the central character:

> In Clym Yeobright's face could be dimly seen the typical countenance of the future. Should there be a classic period to art hereafter, its Pheidias may well produce such faces. The view of life as a thing to be put up with, replacing that zest for existence which was so intense in early civilizations, must ultimately enter so

thoroughly into the constitution of the advanced races that its facial expression will become accepted as a new artistic departure. People already feel that a man who lives without disturbing a curve of feature, or setting a mark of mental concern anywhere upon himself, is too far removed from modern perceptiveness to be a modern type. Physically beautiful men—the glory of the race when it was young—are almost an anachronism now; and we may wonder whether, at some time or other, physically beautiful women may not be an anachronism likewise.

The truth seems to be that a long line of disillusive centuries has permanently displaced the Hellenic idea of life, or whatever it may be called. What the Greeks only suspected, we know well; what their Aeschylus imagined, our nursery children feel. The old-fashioned revelling in the general situation grows less and less possible as we uncover the defects of natural laws, and see the quandary that man is in by their operation.[b]

Of the many points[1] made in this extract, special attention should be given to the final one, which refers to the developments in scientific thought in the nineteenth century: specifically, to the idea of the blind, impersonal workings of natural law, and the problems caused by this process. Such a notion is clearly opposed to Christian doctrine, with its belief in a benignly omnipotent deity. Hardy is in fact one of a group of English writers who were closely in touch with the general movement of ideas in the second half of the nineteenth century: a movement which was actuated to a large extent by scientific discovery, and which was predominantly agnostic or atheistic in character. The gauntness of tone which we find in the Hardy passage is manifest also in the writings of the leading agnostic and atheistic philosophers of the period—who were, as it happens, chiefly German and English. Hardy himself was influenced mainly by Spencer, Schopenhauer and von Hartmann: an influence which, incidentally, he powerfully expressed in an earlier quoted phrase, "the deicide eyes of seers" (in the poem 'A Plaint to Man'). Other major English writers of this period who were highly attuned to philosophical developments include: George Eliot, who derived inspiration from a host of sources, chiefly Spencer, Comte, Feuerbach and Strauss; Matthew Arnold—again subject to a wide range of influences; and, toward the end of the century, Conrad, inspired principally by Schopenhauer.[2]

---

[1] Some are in fact controversial: see endnote b.
[2] As can be seen, Schopenhauer's impact was very widespread at this time, even more so than Spencer's. He was one of the first Western philosophers to be openly atheistic in outlook. Writing in the first half of the nineteenth

Modern Literature: Some Challenges 143

The afore-mentioned gauntness of tone found in the above philosophers was bound up with an intellectually austere and demanding quality which the cultural situation made inevitable: religious faith was either under heavy fire or had been abandoned. Hence, among the intellectually scrupulous, first-hand, rigorous and unevasive thinking was the order of the day. There prevailed a profound sense of the need for intellectual self-accountability and a standing on one's own feet—for, in other words, free thought: a freedom to be maintained and pursued whatever the consequences.

Some of those consequences are detailed in the Irving Howe quotation on Hardy, with which the essay began. They were in Hardy's day, and remain, unavoidable aspects of a post-religious and scientifically committed outlook. That outlook was a challenge to nineteenth century religious and social orthodoxy, and is still one to the social mainstream today.[3] The experience of intellectual crisis, of loneliness and anguish and a sense of the deeply problematic nature of existence, both ontologically and ethically: these are the hallmark features of modernity. They have found their way into most of the major literature of the last 150 years, especially that of twentieth century existentialism.

Overall, the impact of philosophy and science on literature since the mid nineteenth century has been so decisive as to make this period unique in Western culture. Creative writers have always, of course, been open to extraneous influence, since, obviously, they have always been culturally situated. But prior to the nineteenth century, the main cultural influence was religion, which is why the intellectual changes in the nineteenth century were so radical. In a post-religious climate, demonstrable knowledge, scientific discov-

---

century, he deeply influenced its second half, affecting not only English writers but, even more so, Continental ones: the later Tolstoy, and Turgenev, Zola, Maupassant. The international influence extended into the twentieth century, and is most notably evidenced in the writings of Mann and Proust, Beckett and Borges.

Bearing in mind what has been said so far in this essay, a fundamental reason for his resonating so widely is captured in what he says on: "*the problem of existence*—this equivocal, tortured, fleeting, dreamlike existence of ours—so vast and so close that a man no sooner discovers it than it overshadows and obscures all other problems and aims ..." (In *The Essential Schopenhauer*, p. 58)

[3] It should be added that, in countries like Britain, the challenge is not so much to the power of religious institutions as to a mass-outlook which may well have, in the main, rejected religious belief but which is, nevertheless, largely indolent in the philosophical sense, inadequately concerned to explore in depth the implications of agnosticism and atheism.

ery and the ability to argue logically in relation to these things become indispensable, and constitute a genuinely scientific philosophy. In modern times, creative writers of the first rank have been almost universally obliged, in their general thinking, to meet the needs of scientific philosophy, on pain of appearing intellectually fatuous or obsolete. They have had to shoulder the responsibility of endeavouring to encompass what Andre Malraux called the "musee imaginaire" of vast accumulations of knowledge. In no previous period have the intellectual demands on them been so extensive. Barring a future reversion to a religious mentality, this situation appears set to continue.

Agnosticism and atheism, the inevitable sequels to religious belief, have opened up a daunting cosmic perspective. The latter is expressed as succinctly as anywhere in Arnold's previously discussed poem of the mid nineteenth century 'Dover Beach,' where the erstwhile prevalence of religious belief is compared to a sea which surrounds the land "like the folds of a bright girdle furl'd". By contrast, the present decline of faith is likened to the sea's

> melancholy, long, withdrawing roar,
> Retreating, to the breath
> Of the night-wind, down the vast edges drear
> And naked shingles of the world.

This imagery of brute physical facts and forces, and the implication that they are dominant, forcefully convey the idea that the cosmos, viewed without religious belief, is a grim spectacle. Extensions of this perspective are to be found later in the nineteenth century, especially in the work of Hardy and Conrad, and in much twentieth century writing.

Focussing now on the twentieth century, the demise of religious belief has been explicit or at least implicit in the outlooks of a range of major authors. An equally important consideration is that a number of these authors have explored extreme mental suffering as it is encountered outside a framework of religion. For example, when Proust, in the final part of *Remembrance of Things Past*,(1927), avers the symbiotic link between suffering and art, and then argues that "suffering is the best thing one [the artist] can hope to encounter in life",[c] a central place is being assigned to psychological pain in a way that has nothing to do with religious convictions. This is also the case in the work of Beckett (who, incidentally, wrote illuminatingly on Proust). In Beckett's best known play, *Waiting for Godot* (1953), the inescapability of suffering amidst ontological uncertainty is one of the main points to emerge. A similar perspective is to be found in Sartre's novel *Nausea* (1938).

This perspective is also evident in Beckett's fellow practitioners of the Theatre of the Absurd, a major post-1945 movement in drama. These practitioners include Ionesco and Adamov. Ionesco challenges the assumptions which lie beyond a great deal of modern social planning when he says:

> No society has been able to abolish human sadness, no political system can deliver us from the pain of living, from our fear of death, our thirst for the absolute. It is the human condition which directs the social condition, not vice versa.[d]

Adamov, for his part, challenges a number of modern political assumptions connected with goals of economic betterment. He points out that, even if these goals are achieved, mankind will still be faced with ontological questions and perhaps with a sense of alienation from the rest of the cosmos. It is these problems which produce the deepest unhappiness, and they cannot be overcome by economic changes. Specifically on the Communist (we would now be more likely to say 'socialist') project, Adamov wrote in 1946:

> If we turn to Communism ... it is merely because one day, when it will seem quite close to the realisation of its highest aim—the victory over all the contradictions that impede the exchange of goods among men—it will meet, inevitably, the great 'no' of the nature of things, which it thought it could ignore in its struggle.
>
> When the great obstacles are overcome, when man will no longer be able to deceive himself as to the nature of his unhappiness, there will arise an anxiety all the more powerful, all the more fruitful for being stripped of anything that might have hindered its realisation.[e]

Adamov's reference to the "great 'no' of the nature of things" was actually anticipated by Forster in his novel *A Passage to India* (1924). In this novel, Forster dramatically explores the view that human values have no meaning or significance, in any objective sense, beyond the human sphere—one which is miniscule in comparison to the rest of the cosmos. Such a viewpoint leads to the idea of the 'otherness' of the outer universe, to the latter's utter differentness from all that human beings cherish.[4] This indeed is Adamov's "great 'no'". Forster's concomitant point—that "Everything exists" but that

---

[4] For a leading expression of this outlook in twentieth century poetry, see the work of Robert Frost, about which the critic Randall Jarrell writes: "the limits which existence approaches and falls back from have seldom been stated with such bare composure."

"nothing has value"[f] (meaning an objective value as distinct from a human-subjective one) — is closely related to modern atheistic existentialism, and also to the non-objectivist school of thought in ethical philosophy. Further, like Ionesco's and Adamov's positions, it is a riposte to those elements of homocentric complacency which underlie so much modern social and political thought.

It perhaps goes without saying that modern literature is such a vast area that the full range of challenges it presents to superficial mentalities cannot possibly be covered in the space of a short essay like this one. As said in the introduction, my aim has been to examine only some of those challenges. At the same time, I have selected those which seem to me to be representative, in that they show literature's connection with philosophy and science: a connection which, as I have argued, is unparalleled in its extent, and which therefore constitutes a distinctive feature of modern imaginative writing. In the modern world, no writer can be major unless s/he has trodden, some way at least, the rocky uphill terrain that is post-religious philosophy and science. That hard journey is a pivotal experience for all those who undertake it, and involves — again — the doubts and crises to which Howe refers in the introductory quotation.

Nonetheless, in contrast to what Howe says, these problems need not be permanent; or, alternatively, they need not persist at high pitch or remain the central feature of consciousness. Problems can be resolved or at least reduced. Where they have produced crisis, a later, more sustainable psychological position lies on the other side of crisis. The movement to the other side of the formidably problematic — a movement free, of course, of false certainties — seems to me to be among the most significant kinds of psychic regeneration that modern literature describes. One of the most vivid examples of this transition is in Sartre's play *The Flies* (1942), where a leading character, Orestes, affirms that "human life begins on the far side of despair".[g] Another powerful instance is in Somerset Maugham's novel *Of Human Bondage* (1915), where the central character, Philip, comes to regard existence as essentially chaotic, without any moral structure or value in an objective sense,[5] but then begins to view the pain and unhappiness which arise from this chaos, and which have dogged his own personal life, in a new and wholly detached way — a way which is philosophically liberating.[h]

---

[5] This notion that existence lacks objective moral value has clear links with what has previously been said about Forster's *A Passage to India,* and about atheistic existentialism.

Modern Literature: Some Challenges 147

In summary: the morally positive positions which leading modern writers have reached have been hard-won in the highest degree, the product of radical intellectual searching and of open engagement[i] with the enormous complexity of modern thought. The latter has increasingly taken the form of scientific philosophy, and engagement with it has increasingly led to positions which are agnostic or atheistic. This situation appears likely to continue in Western culture — continue and deepen, and therefore present further challenges to outlooks which are superficial, perfunctory, unself-critical and indolent. Experience thus far suggests that these outlooks will persist, and that, therefore, there will continue to be enormous oppositional tasks for the creative mind to perform.

End Notes

[a] Publication details were given in the essay on Matthew Arnold.
[b] *The Return of the Native* (London: Macmillan, 1965 (1878)), p. 174. However, what Hardy says about Greek culture is questionable. Though he does refer to the tragedian Aeschylus, he gives, on this occasion, insufficient attention to Greek tragic drama. The latter was a crucial part of the "Hellenic" outlook to which he refers: a point that was cogently made by Hardy's German contemporary, Nietzsche, in *The Birth of Tragedy*, published in 1872, six years before *The Return of the Native*. Hence the Greeks more than "suspected" the existence of the dark areas of experience; their outlook was extremely complex, and a "revelling in the general situation" was not its predominant feature.
[c] *Remembrance of Things Past*, Vol. 12, trans. Andreas Mayor (London: Chatto and Windus, 1970 (1927)), p. 281
[d] As quoted by Martin Esslin in *The Theatre of the Absurd* (Penguin Bks., 1976 (1961)), pp. 126-7.
[e] *Ibid.*, pp. 93-4.
[f] *A Passage to India* (Penguin Bks., 1963 (1924)), p. 147.
[g] In *'The Flies and 'In Camera'*, trans. Stuart Gilbert (London: Hamish Hamilton, 1958 (1946)), p. 97.
[h] *Of Human Bondage* (Penguin Bks., 1963 (1915)), pp. 525-6.
[i] As an incidental point, this general engagement is nowhere better exemplified than in the novels of Thomas Mann. His fiction is perhaps unsurpassed in its intellectual density: one of the factors which made him the most critically discussed writer of the twentieth century.

Index of Names

Adamov, Arthur 145-6
Aeschylus 138, 147
Allen, Walter 16
Anouilh, Jean 139
Aristotle 33
Arnold, Matthew 86, 113, 127-36, 142, 144
Austen, Jane 35

Beckett, Samuel 131, 139, 143-4
Bergson, Henri 58, 84
Berlin, Isaiah 34, 122
Blackham, Harold 121
Bloom, Harold 35
Borges, Luis 143
Brecht, Bertolt 2
Browning, Robert 127, 135

Camus, Albert 34
Carlyle, Thomas 14, 113
Cervantes, Miguel de 33
Chekhov, Anton 32
Chomsky, Noam 13
Christ 2
Coleridge, S.T. 113
Comte, Auguste 82, 112-20, 122-3, 142
Confucius 15
Conrad, Joseph 131. 144
Corneille, Pierre 137

D'Alembert, Jean 32
Dante 25, 33, 85
Darwin, Charles 51, 55, 59, 68, 72, 74, 79, 84, 129
Dawkins, Richard 72-3
DaVinci, Leonardo 41
Democritus 83
Dewey, John 83, 89
D'Holbach, Baron 32
Dickens, Charles 25, 35
Diderot, Denis 32
Dostoyevsky, Fyodor 32
Durkheim, Émile 29, 112-13, 117-18, 120, 122-3

Eliot, T.S. 6, 118
Euripides 138

Feuerbach, Ludwig 82, 142
Forster, E.M. 22, 34, 140, 145-6
Freud, Sigmund 58, 118
Frost, Robert 145

Gide, Andre 45
Goethe, Wolfgan 25, 85, 137g
Gogol, Nicholai 32
Greene, Graham 131

Hardy, Thomas 79, 85-8, 130, 141-2, 144, 147
Hegel, G.F.W. 83
Heidegger, Martin 120, 123
Heisenberg, Werner 73
Hobbes, Thomas 36, 70
Howe, Irving 130, 141
Hume, David 36, 58-9, 67, 75, 117, 122

Ibsen, Henrik 86, 137
Ionesco, Eugene 145-6

James, Henry 16-18, 25
Jarrell, Randall 145
Joyce, James 140
Jung, C.G. 118

Kant, Immanuel 70, 115, 129

Lucretius 85

Magee, Bryan 73
Malraux, Andre 5, 144
Mann, Thomas 143, 147
Marlowe, Christopher 137
Marx, Karl 6-7, 14, 16, 82, 89, 112-13, 117, 120-1, 124
Maugham, Somerset 131, 146
Maupassant, Guy 143
Mendel, Gregor 72
Mill, J.S. 3, 94-7
Milton, John 25
Morris, William 9

Nader, Ralph 13
Napoleon 32-3

Index of Names

Nietzsche, F.W. 3, 14, 53, 58-9, 66, 82, 94-7, 119, 147
O'Neill, Eugene 139

Orwell, George 20

Pareto, Vilfredo 6, 58, 118
Plato 15, 25
Pope, Alexander 25
Popper, Karl 5-6, 29, 34, 44, 49, 120, 124
Proust, Marcel 33, 143-4
Pushkin, Alexander 32

Racine, Jean 137, 139
Rousseau, J.J. 32
Russell, Bertrand 34, 44-5, 60, 78-84, 89, 91, 123-4

Santayana, George 6, 14, 27, 58, 63-4, 79-80, 82-92, 118, 120
Sartre, J.P. 76, 89, 120, 122, 130-1, 145-6
Schopenhauer, Arthur 6, 58, 65-77, 82-3, 85, 88-92, 115-16, 129, 142-3

Shakespeare, William 6, 25, 33, 35, 119, 135, 137-9
Socrates 67-8, 71
Sophocles 33, 138-9
Spencer, Herbert 82, 89, 112, 142
Spengler, Oswald 11-15
Spinoza, Baruch 40, 65, 80
Stalin, Josef 32, 104, 124
Strauss, David

Tennyson, Alfred 127, 129, 135
Thomson, James 78-9
Tolstoy, Leo 32, 143
Toynbee, Arnold 12
Turgenev, Ivan 32, 143

Voltaire 25, 32

Weber, Max 120-6
Wells, H.G. 14
Williams, Raymond 9
Williams, Tennessee 131, 139
Wordsworth, William 123

Zola, Emile 143